THE TWENTY-FIRST-CENTURY GOSPEL OF JESUS CHRIST

AS TOLD TO

JO ANN LEVITT

THE TWENTY-FIRST-CENTURY GOSPEL OF JESUS CHRIST

TRANSCRIBED AND EDITED BY

JO ANN LEVITT

Library of Congress Control Number:		2019920729
ISBN:	Hardcover	978-1-7960-7892-3
	Softcover	978-1-7960-7893-0
	eBook	978-1-7960-7894-7

Print information available on the last page.

Rev. date: 12/19/2019

To order additional copies of this book, contact:
Xlibris
1-888-795-4274
www.Xlibris.com
Orders@Xlibris.com
805971

CONTENTS

Introduction

Sitting in a small chapel on a mountaintop in Southern France in September of 2019, I was fortunate to be meditating with a small group of people who had joined together for an unusual spiritual journey. During the ten days of our vision quest, we had received powerful personal guidance, had had soulful encounters, and had shared many deep meditative experiences in a gathering that was called Divine Light Activation, guided by Danielle Rama Hoffman.

On that particular morning, engrossed in the quiet of St. Salvarre Chapel, I fell into a deep trance state. For long moments, I was completely stationary and without thought. Then suddenly what passed before my eyes was a banner-like image or scroll with these words written across: *The Twenty-First-Century Gospel of Jesus Christ.* At first, I wasn't sure what it meant. (I mean, I understood the words, but not their relevance to me.) Little by little, it dawned on me that I was being asked to take up my pen and paper and write a new Gospel. Extraordinary invitation! No sooner had that thought occurred than I found myself seated in meditation later that day, with words pouring in—words I might never have conjured or dreamed up on my own but, nevertheless, words that prompted me to begin writing without question. From that moment on, I would receive a block of ideas, usually preceded by a brief title, such as "Contemplation" or "Praise," or occasionally something longer, such as "What Does It Mean to Co-create?" and I would continue the intensively focused writing, word for word.

As I had never channeled or done any kind of automatic writing before, this was all new to me and quite surprising. But from the first chapter to the last, there was hardly a pause in the process. Every morning, new thoughts, insights, questions, and responses to them came forth from Jesus and filled these pages.

Once I had begun writing, I became enchanted—you could almost say obsessed—with its completion. Everything else dulled in comparison, and the scribing seemed to follow me everywhere I went. On leaving France and returning home to the States, I found myself in a whirlwind of channeled activity. For a full month, I could not think or do anything unless it was related to setting down Jesus' thoughts. Often, I'd wake up at 3:00 a.m. to write or, conversely, sit right down upon returning home from work. For the first time in living memory, meals became unimportant to me, or at least subservient to the task of scribing; and I felt absolutely committed to completing the project. It had taken on a life of its own.

The result is what you see here. To me, it is certainly Good News, which is how we generally translate the meaning of **Gospel**. However, the interesting thing to note (toward the end of this work) is that Christ wants us **all** to provide updates. He wants us all to share in the writing, the revelation, and the renewed experience of living the Gospels wholeheartedly. So this is one result. It seems to fit with Twenty-First-Century ideas and experience. And as he often said to his disciples, "Come and see."

The Twenty-First-Century Gospel

1. Jesus Begins

I invite you to join me wholeheartedly in these pages and, for a brief moment, suspend your disbelief about what you find here. Although it may seem to you that I've been silent through the course of these past two thousand years, in actuality, that's not true. I have been actively engaged and communicative, but not so much on the larger stage as with one Soul at a time. I have been conversing with you in dreams. I have answered questions you were brave enough to ask and even some you felt too shy to put forth. I have been with you in houses of prayer, in temples, in churches, on beaches, on mountaintops, and while crossing the seas. But the time is ripe now for me to speak out in language you can access and understand.

Many folks are amazed or dumbfounded when we Ancients return and speak in modern parlance. Of course, you won't find me on Facebook or Twitter, but you will hear me refer to modern people, places, and events. Sometimes I'll even engage in less-than-righteous language. I realize it can be jarring, but that's only because you expect me to step right out of the King James Version of the Bible or the NRSV (New Revised Standard Version). Some may even hold on to the image of me as a prophet or shepherd, dressed in robes, eating locusts and honey, like my cousin John the Baptist.

But consider then how narrow your definition of *omniscience* must be. Again, it's due to an inherent flaw in your understanding of Light Beings. You see, we are all Light Beings, whether we're in form or in the Light. Either way, our bodies and energies are woven out of Light itself. And just because I'm not in form does not mean that I am not present. I have been deeply engaged with you for more than two thousand years and even beyond that, so I'm fully up-to-date on current events, global concerns, changes in language, culture, clothing, morals, music—everything. Your idea that I'm somehow still "back there" in time is not applicable. Please do me a great favor and bring me to the present, here and now! I should hope that, after all these years, I've become eligible for an upgrade in my "operating system," from a mere 2.0 to 2020 or higher!

You can view this text as part of re-visioning process—an evolution of the older texts. A funny idea occurred, or if you will, a play on my own words. I have not come to kill off the texts of Matthew, Mark, Luke, or John, but rather to *fulfill* them. I have come to reinterpret them for this age, to revise, to reinvigorate, and to breathe new life into the corpus. But this work exists outside of the framework of ordinary time, as you know it, as do I, and as do many other Light Beings in Light. We do not live on the Earthly plane, but we exist as a huge halo, if you will—a gathering of Divine Lights surrounding the globe, sparking new life, new energy, and helping the Old Paradigm disassemble itself to midwife and make way for the Paradigm of Love.

As far as how this work has been produced, it's quite simple. I speak to my editor, Jo Ann, in the course of her daily meditations, and she writes down what she hears me say. We call her a scribe. I've been conversing with her for years, but this is the first time she's had the courage to bring forth our communications in written form.

Because I am presenting a few different ideas or interpretations from those that were originally presented by the four Evangelists, bear with me. As you receive new facts or a new light on the old subjects, let your mind stretch a bit to take in the information. Allow it to show up as the latest chapter in your knowledge of the Gospels. After all, there were quite a few Gospels written in the same era that, for one reason or another, never got included in the full canon (that is, the *approved* contents of your current Bible).

If you have doubts about the authenticity of what's scribed, no worries! Just stay tuned and check with your own inner knowing. There are concepts you'll resonate with and others that you won't. Just be careful not to work so hard authenticating what's here that you miss the essential message. And finally, recognize that even though you live in a very evidence-based culture, there's still plenty of *data* that defies your scientific methods. So be of good cheer. Enjoy yourself, and if you choose, allow me to whisper to you in your dreams or in your heart or on these pages. In so many ways, I'll be telling you how much you are loved!

2. The Paradigm of Love

This is not news for most of you. However, I've changed some of the language to be more respectful of the time and to be "PC," as you call it. You will recall how much I spoke of the Kingdom of Heaven, in Matthew. It's too bad folks saw that as a realm far removed from Earth and even from the natural course of a lifetime. Even though I kept repeating myself, murmuring "The Kingdom of God is near," so many of the disciples took that to mean "It's on its way; take heed." And because they wanted a King so badly, they saw it as a change in government, not a change in consciousness. My bad. I had to use the language that made sense at the time, but I apologize for the ensuing confusion. Even when I claimed the Kingdom was within you, that didn't land as intended.

It's not just that God is within you or that you can reach out for occasional tastes of the sublime. You are the Sublime. You are the Infinite and Eternal One yourself; you are God incarnate. How heretical of me to proclaim such a thing, I who've been the Wonder Boy of flesh incarnate. But you will have to take some time to let go of the Kingdom so you can enter the new Paradigm. Hard to envision? That's because you've been trying so hard to *get* somewhere. You've been ringing bells and burning incense for centuries, damning the witches and crowning the bishops. None of that belongs to me, and like our old Pop Jehovah once said in Scripture, "I have no need of your burnt offerings." So don't bring your calves or your pigeons, your sheep or your doves, or anything else you feel you must offer in order to justify your existence. Your life is *enough*. Use it in service to your own precious Divine Nature and to the God in you and me and the whole planet. All these centuries, you've been bowing to ghosts. The real Spirit Beings and the real Deities live right under your hat. They're hiding out in your belly. They tickle inside your fingertips, and above all, they speak through your heartstrings. Listen. "Here am I. Have you searched for me, Dear One? Why go so far? I'm the breath between breaths. I'm your very next heartbeat. I am whom you've searched for, and isn't it uncanny how many disguises popped up so that you couldn't find me? Well, now you see me as I am. Embrace me in your mirror. Shake hands with God."

3. What It Means to Live in the Paradigm of Love

Much like the myths of the Kingdom of God, living in the Paradigm of Love does not mean love happens outside of you or on some distant planet. When I said "Love your neighbor as yourself," people argued over the meaning of it for centuries. Does it mean I can't love others until I love myself? Who comes first? Me or my neighbor? A simple sutra suddenly got wound into a thousand knots. If you and your neighbor are ONE, what does it matter whom you love first?

Living in the Paradigm of Love means no one is less than or more than, and everyone is automatically related. *Vasudhaiva Kutumbakam*— the Whole world is One Family. So creed, color, caste, or nationality makes no difference; we're in this together. And everyone, without exception, is entitled to everyone else's love. But let's do away with the word *entitlement* because it has the word *title* in it. It's not just that you extend love or you receive love. Go deeper. Go down into the bedrock and through to the steam of love that forms the very essence of your being. You are Love. I am Love. We are Love. No one doubts that we need air to breathe. No one doubts that we need blood circulating to nourish our bodies. We live in the exchange of air to blood to breath and back again. Like air and blood, Love itself is a vital link to survival. It's getting pumped through our system every minute, every hour, and yet we recognize its flow about as often as we stop to notice we're breathing.

If Love is your very essence—what you're made of, what you exude, and what you must take in in order to survive—then it's no wonder half the planet walks around starving and airless. Just like insomniacs are sleep-deprived, others live in a love *deficit*, Love-deprived. Everyone keeps yelling "Hydrate, hydrate!" but now they should be saying "Vacate, vacate!" Give up being so enclosed in your tiny, small self that you miss the opportunity for a vital love exchange—a full ventilation of your living organism.

How many ways can you find to actively love others? How many ways can you accept and graciously receive the love others offer you? How often can you love and honor yourself, especially when you've screwed up? The church talks about the giving of your time, talent, and treasure, but that often amounts to just a small trickle, while you have a veritable River of Love—no, an Ocean of Love—available. Invent Love. Create Love. Investigate Love. Champion Love. Let Love define you, refine you, revise you, advise you, conspire with you, aspire through you, inspire you, and surprise you. Let Love come as Revelation. Let Love be the means to your Transformation. Be Love unceasingly, and let Love breathe through you, lighting up your very being through its Divine fire.

4. Consider the Lilies of the Field

They neither toil nor spin. You, my precious lilies, need toil no longer. Bloom. Blossom. Delight in life, for your fragrance wafts through the air and draws in all the little bees. *Buzz, buzz, buzz.* Everywhere you are, there is so much nectar, so much honey; you are dripping with the nectar of loving, giving, and receiving, and all this precious honey forms a comb that each one takes and eats and that nourishes right down to the bone and through to the Soul.

You immortalized those words that I spoke on the occasion of the Last Supper: "This is my body; take and eat in remembrance of me," when I offered up the bread, and "This is the cup of the new covenant," when I offered up the wine. "Take and drink in remembrance of me." Instead of arguing over whether you were eating my actual flesh or drinking my blood, why not see that I was asking you to be in *Communion* with me? Not eating or drinking but rather living and loving. Whoever sits at your table is part of your family, so now stretch the table, lengthen it out, and broaden it so it encompasses the whole world. Everyone, come sit down. Take and eat. Take and drink. Join the New Communion, which offers only one meal we take in common; that is the nourishment we receive when sharing our infinite love and devotion to one another and spreading it throughout the world.

5. How Is It That We Co-create?

Although it may seem strange for me to bring her into this text, you must know that my editor, Jo Ann, asked this question many times. She wanted better understanding of the Cocreation that may occur between Light Beings in Light and Light Beings on Earth. In a way, it's too bad that none of the Evangelists gave me a chance to get a word in edgewise, but then you must realize that they wrote their Gospels after I'd departed. For that matter, some of them never even knew me in the flesh.

However, beneath Jo Ann's question—"Can we actually work with you and cocreate together?"—was a deeper question. She questioned her own abilities and, beneath that, her *deservingness*. "How can I possibly be elected to cocreate with you, Oh magnificent Lord?" That is not such an unusual response, given the context of the Old Paradigm, in which we had Lords and Kings and those we do homage to. Or at the other end of the spectrum, think about the Sudras, outcasts in India, or the lepers, the possessed, or the so-called unclean in ancient Israel.

You see, as we evolve in consciousness as a human race, we must first sort out, contrast, and distinguish who we are from everyone else (or how exceedingly different we are from the apes). To know what light is, we need to contrast it with darkness. Hot reminds us of cold, and wet needs an ocean rather than a desert. These opposites help us understand the nature of duality, which always has two opposing poles. What we fail to understand, however, more than the fact that opposites attract, is that in the end, opposites *combine* and fold back into the Oneness.

However, living in duality does not mean living in separation, nor does it mean I'm better than you or you're better than me. This was one of the hardest things for Jo Ann to accept—that she and I are equal. She still wavers on this point. Nevertheless, it is axiomatic: you and I are equal; everyone born into human form is equal. That does not mean we have equal skills or heritage, and certainly, it does not signify equal opportunity. It does not even mean we are equally evolved. However, think about a six-year-old in first grade versus a sixteen-year-old in high school. You would not consider them unequal, but rather, in different stages of their development. That is true for everyone; we are all equal because we are One in Spirit, One in Source. We all emerge from the same *Prima Materia*; we all have access to and partake of Spirit. And at the level of Spirit, there is no differentiation. Can you separate a wave from the ocean? Can the sky above be partitioned into separate units?

The one who looks outward sees only differences. But for the one who looks within, she sees only that which unifies. So how do you Look within? First, you must stop and breathe. Then understand that it has to do with attention and, equally, with intention. You create an intention to know yourself as Divine, to know yourself at the level of Soul, at the Source of Life. But to penetrate in such a way takes more than a token thought or a token breath or even a token pause. You must be willing to set aside all preoccupation with time—time passing, time for To-Dos, being on time, in time, or out of time.

Enter the timeless state. Breathe. Relax. Then turn your focus to your innermost thoughts and your innermost heartbeat. There you will meet up with your innermost breath. At that crossroads, you will depart from external distractions and come to the still point at the eye of the storm, the point where Silence reigns. There you and I will easily come to meet. And when we come together, that marks a turning point, for now we are joined in the work of Spirit. Now we can collaborate on any kind of undertaking that fulfills our Spiritual mission. But don't get me wrong. It's not only I who cocreates with you. You have the entire Pantheon of Light beings at your disposal. Whom are you called to work with? Isis, Osiris, my dear brother Thoth, Mother Mary or the Magdalenes, Shiva or Buddha, Muhammad, or Melchizedek? There are millions more. Cocreation joins our efforts and intentions, both as Light Beings incarnate and Light Beings in Light, so that we have even greater impact working together. And all along you thought you had to do this alone!

6. Why I Speak Now in This Language

You are aware that English is not my native tongue. So everything being translated is in the language most suitable to my scribe, i.e., the one she learned growing up. However, with a few exceptions, your Bible does not record my spoken Aramaic tongue. What a pity! It had nuances even Hebrew couldn't capture. And then to turn everything into Greek is clearly *Greek* to me. Yet Greek was the predominant tongue, and through that language, the Evangelists—mainly Luke and John—could disseminate the narrative more easily and more rapidly. In like manner, since English is more widely spoken around the world today, I chose Jo Ann to record this Gospel.

Since I am not currently incarnate, I do not speak any earthly language. For the most part, Light Beings speak in the languages of Light, which is where the world of Light, Sound, and Idea intersect. It is, in a sense, a shorthand version of your lengthier form of communication through words. You may not realize it, but it takes a long time to translate thoughts into words. When Jo Ann receives an *etheric download* from me, it comes in a kind of big clump—a combined thought, picture, and series of words all chunked together—like a package just received from UPS. But instead of tearing off the tape or cutting through flaps to open the box, she moves in the opposite direction. Little by little, one word after another, she begins to reassemble the box. If she could speak in Light Language, of course, it would be easier. But that's for another time. For now, the scribing proceeds in a beautiful flow. A true scribe (and many of you fit this description) holds the consciousness of herself, the narrator (in this case, me), and the audience all in one organic, well-combined whole. Essentially, there's no distinction among any of the three, for as I will tell you often enough, we are all in this together.

7. About My Ministry

I really like the fact that the two words *ministry* and *mystery* are nearly interchangeable. Since *ministry* comes from the root word *ministerium*, it sounds quite familiar, doesn't it? However, it refers to "one who serves." This can take on several meanings. I could serve in a church or be an agent of government (as so many would have preferred). But the simpler version of ministry, which is to be a servant of the people, refers best to my brief time on earth.

As Matthew observed, I came to teach and help redefine righteousness. As Mark observed, I came to change the narrative and shake people up a bit. As Luke observed, I came to heal and care for others—especially those disenfranchised—and I came to pray. John would add that I was here before Adam and that I came to light up the path, the truth, and the way. While all these things were—in some measure—true, I came to fulfill my own dharma: to evolve in my spiritual being and open new channels of communication with the world. In a sense, what you are reading now is just one step further along the chain of acts and communications that mark my gift to the world and, simultaneously, the unfolding of my dharma.

You see, we never stop evolving. We all continue to expand, take in new ideas, and move out into this and other worlds, armed with new knowledge and capabilities. Or did you think wisdom was confined only to Earth? You, too, may have had your home on Neptune or Sirius or the Pleiades. In every place we inhabit, we are sharpening our skills in communication and collaboration, experimenting with the collective dream with and for one another.

Earth is a newer experiment, and now the energy is coalescing; more light and greater consciousness are coming through. So you could say that my *Ministry* is to help introduce a new design for living based on the Paradigm of Love. However, I would be remiss if I didn't also acknowledge the amazing group of Souls who landed here with me in that prior incarnation. Together we carried on our Light work; together we carried out our combined ministries and brought them to all corners of the Earth. Besides the twelve whom you know so well, I also wish to acknowledge the immense gratitude and love I feel for the often behind-the-scenes workers, such as Anna; my mother, Mary; Mary Magdalene and many of the Magdalene enclave (including Susanna, Lydia, Salome, and Priscilla); and Joseph, my father, as well as Lazarus, Nicodemus, and Joseph of Arimathea. There were many others, too numerous to mention, but I remember and love them all.

You will probably get tired of hearing me say it, but I could never have accomplished what I did on my own. I had many helpers on this plane and many Light Beings of Light looking on and whispering their support.

It is too bad the events of my life came to be summarized as tragedy. They did not occur in the way you imagined, but rather, as a Divine Experiment of Light. Seeds were planted on the Earth then that have been germinating over the course of the past two thousand years. Now their shoots have popped up, and soon the Earth will witness their sheer beauty as She blossoms fully into Love.

8. Get a New Prescription for Your Glasses

If you're having trouble seeing the world from the lens of Unity, then you may need to adjust your vision or get help in scrolling down from duality to Oneness. It's so easy to make a case for conflict. It's so easy to fight or struggle. In the old Power-Over or Power-Under experience, you had to fight for your rights, prove you were better than others, and snuff out any contenders for your goods and position. Yet times have changed, and you will need new glasses and a new way of seeing if you are to accept this New Paradigm of Love.

As a matter of fact, it's not as *new* as you might think; it's been around for eons. But we go in and out of conscious connection, or "in and out the window," as the children's song suggests. What brings us the awakening? For many, it's a question of timing and preparation. You will remember that when my mother mentioned that the wine had run out at Cana, I told her it was not yet my *time*. I did not feel I could summon sufficient power at that stage of my growth to make a difference for the wedding party; however, Mary's vision went much deeper. Lucky for the guests, they got to drink their fill because of her vision.

The healing process is also based on a vision of Unity. When I saw a blind man or a leper, I was able to focus on their wholeness and their unified state of being, which when reflected back to them, in a sense, helped restore their own *vision*. It is a process of up-leveling your vibrational stance so you see the whole being, the whole picture, and the whole context, and you see everything from a place of instant Love and connection. Your very sight restores order.

In Unity consciousness, you are the Healer, the Creator, the Unifier, and the Weaver—your sight itself weaves back apparently disparate parts of life into their original Divine plan and wholeness. The web of life has all things interconnected, as your great Dr. Martin Luther King Jr. once proclaimed: "We are made to live together by the very nature of reality itself."

9. In and Out

There are indeed times when you fall in and out of love. There are times when someone's neglect or lack of interest in you or jarring comments make you feel like an outsider or unworthy of love. Or perhaps something in their anger or judgment has you shutting down. These are natural events, and these move through us, almost like taking in a breath and then exhaling. However, there is something noteworthy about this Separation consciousness. You actually *feel* separate, as if you've been exiled from your tribe or family and exiled from the sense of safety and inclusion you normally experience. But in truth, you're not outside of anything. It's just that you've stepped away from yourself. Energetically, you've created separation from your own Source. Now it's impossible to literally *separate*, but there is a way that we wander outside the fold, like proverbial lost sheep. To be found, however, means we must first find ourselves and find our way back into Union so we are reconnected—body, mind, Soul, and Universe. Of course, no one left. No one arrived. All along, you've been sitting in the seat of Pure Consciousness but forgot to check your seat number.

10. Compassion

Everyone has her own ideas about compassion. Often, it seems easier to indulge this virtue than the broader, more mysterious, and sometimes vague ideal we refer to as Love. Yet compassion is no easy thing. It requires the greatest act of selflessness. To be truly compassionate is to abandon the "fortress of the Self," as Carlos Castaneda reminds us.

To step outside of our own narrow perspective and for once experience the world as another person does is not easy. For us to let go, even for a few moments, of our own precious point of view, in many cases, feels unsafe and disturbing. However, being compassionate calls for an act of true courage, and in case your French is lacking, courage comes in its original package, combined with the word *Coeur or Heart*.

Above all, compassion takes Heart. The Heart has always been able to feel beyond its own boundaries. The Heart is tapped into the breath, the heartbeat, and the emotions of those around us, as well as within us; it always has been and always will. Meanwhile, the Mind guards its own turf jealously, in effect saying, "No one threatens my reality." Whereas the province of the Mind is to declare its thoughts original and without equal, the province of the Heart is to declare all people's thoughts and feelings original, authentic, and worthy of being listened to and understood. And if you are willing to go the extra mile, then engaging true compassion means you *feel with* that other person. Think about this. If you are really available to *feel with* someone else, what it means is that you have had the courage to dive into and *feel* your own pain and suffering first and eventually accept or come to terms with it. Experiencing compassion for another is no different from walking a mile in their moccasins or living their life experience as your own, without necessarily collapsing in sorrow or fright at their dilemma. It does not even mean that you agree or accept their position; instead, it means you sense what they feel and how they came to feel what they do, and in a certain way, you *suffer* with them. Your heart stretches wide and deep to encompass their heart—to hold them in your embrace and to send them the energy of acceptance, peace, and tender loving-kindness.

His Holiness the Dalai Lama has offered a beautiful set of prayers and instructions that are available for everyone interested in the practice of compassion. If you search his extensive offerings, you may find words that are a match for you and that align with your own vision and longing for compassion in the world. Briefly summarized, he asks that you make three statements, each one directed to someone different: the first applies to yourself, the second to another being, and the third goes out to the whole world. There are many variations on this theme; however, this is the practice in a nutshell:

> May I be happy.
> May you be happy.
> May all beings know happiness.

We can also add these words to express our hope for compassion:

> May I rest within the compassionate heart of God.
> May you rest within the compassionate heart of God.
> May all beings rest within the compassionate heart of God.

11. You Have Heard It Said …

You will often hear my words introduced that way in Matthew's Gospel, especially in the section known as the Beatitudes. It is a useful device for creating contrast: first, the old rule is stated, and then it is contrasted with an update or a newer version. For example, when I say "Love your neighbor and hate your enemies," I add "Love your enemies as well" or "Turn your cheek if you are struck" or "Give someone your overcoat if they ask for your coat." In other words, don't resist those who would resist you. Be at peace with conflict. While John's Gospel goes back to the very beginning, starting out with the poetic words from Genesis, "In the Beginning was the word," in Mark's Gospel, we skip beginnings entirely. You are plunged right into the scene when I meet John the Baptist at the Jordan River. Luke focuses on a different audience, remarking on the presence of the people, the disenfranchised, the poor, and at the same time, the *amazement* of those witnessing the events.

Each Gospel has similarities, naturally. They are representing one life, one era, and one series of events. However, since each Evangelist was writing at a different time and focusing on a different group of people, there were built-in differences. The greatest variation, however, came from the nature of their own personalities, what they treasured, what they valued, and the particular vantage point from which they witnessed or relied on other witnesses to recount those events.

Now imagine you're at Fenway Park. There's a huge commotion because it's the Red Sox playing the New York Yankees. You blew a month's salary to get the best seats, so you have a front-row version of the game and can recount everything nearly verbatim when you return home. (We won't divulge who won.) Once home, you tell your story. Meanwhile, another version with commentary shows up in the *Boston Globe*. However, when you happen to read *the New York Times,* you're amazed how much adoration is shown for the Yankees and how little for the Red Sox. But everyone has a point of view. Even if you sat through the game, your narrative would be affected by your position and whether you were seated in a section loyal to your team or opposed.

Nowadays, you can catch snippets of the game on TV or the Internet. Frankly, I'm happy such technology was not available during my time on earth. Imagine what it would be like if I made the front page of the *Times:* Jesus Trashes the Temple. Then someone catches me on their iPhone, and in ten minutes, the shots go viral of me throwing out cages, clearing tables of merchandise, or yelling at the profiteers. Meanwhile, other people post images of folks getting healed or receiving fish and chunks of bread to eat while we're up on the mountain. Whose story do you subscribe to? Which point of view is preferred? You're getting the basic idea—whatever is deemed most important in the moment gets captured on text or tape or tablet. And if you did not personally witness the event, then you must rely on others' testimony.

That is how the different reports and variations came through the Gospels. Whereas now you have incredible and often relentless visual cues and reminders, in those early days, communication was essentially via word of mouth. Then the text got recorded afterward, but rarely in play-by-play action during the event itself. So read with that in mind and trust your own heart to discern what in fact happened of importance and what is relevant to your inner development now. Whatever leads you on the path to the Living God is the Gospel of choice, particularly if it aids in the uncovering of the Divine within you and with *You* as the Divine.

12. Gathering as Disciples

You will recall that in Mark, Matthew, and Luke, I called the disciples one by one, starting with Andrew and Peter and then calling out the sons of Zebedee, until all twelve were assembled. What didn't get recounted, however, was the fact that all twelve had called on me first. There was a request—a plea. They may not have known me directly, but they were reaching out for help from beyond. Levi, in particular, had a strong urge for new teachings; being a tax collector was never enough. So I came. But remember that you summoned me; all of you summoned me. I would never have come without the invitation. Why else do you think those fishermen dropped their nets? They had been calling and asking and thinking, "There's more to life than this."

I regret that you had to clothe me in such lofty words and ethereal visions. Of course, it's part of the Old Paradigm of Over and under, Better and worse, or Higher and lower. The different perspectives recounted in the Bible are each very helpful; however, some got lost in rhetoric or the desire to compare *teams*, playing favorites. In some cases, it would have been helpful to dumb it down a bit, to look at the combined role of teacher, preacher, and healer as effecting one thing only—alignment.

If you wanted to learn geometry, for example, you'd find a good math teacher. If you wanted to play guitar, you wouldn't seek a piano teacher or a car mechanic; you'd seek someone with the appropriate skills and knowledge. I came to share with you the secret of internal alignment or Sacred concordance—the will to be present as Divine and share in the experience of the Divine, to come home to your True Home even while on Earth, and to share with all of us Light Beings your own indwelling Light-conceived Self.

I did not come for you to worship me. If you cast me in this godlike role, then surely you would understand that a god—if she be a true God—has no need of worship. What she needs instead is Cocreation—sharing in the act of creation. It's not the Old Man on a cloud calling things into existence by uttering a few words. It's all of us working together, joining our thoughts, hopes, and visions, which blend into a new reality. We've been working with you all along, and occasionally we call in our Team—a strong working group—to incarnate on the Earthly plane for specific tasks and forward momentum. But we're not sectioned off into silos between earth and spirit, as you might have imagined.

Sharing the act of Cocreation is what *lights* up Light Beings everywhere. When we work together, we call in many new varieties of form and structure, many new experiences. Think of it: If you only worshipped me, what does the world receive? And if I live already in the pure, positive space of the Divine, what is it that I need? Nothing at all, Dear Ones, nothing at all.

But your will to worship is pure and powerful; you need to channel its energies and lasso them back into the space around and within you so that all you see and all you touch is transmuted into and emerges from that blessed space of Love. Worship in your service to your own growth, and I am with you. Worship in your service to others, and I am with you. Worship to recall and revisit the Divine, of which you are already a part. St. Teresa of Avila wrote a beautiful poem in which she said, "Christ has no body now but yours." These are powerful words, but not exactly the whole truth. In Cocreation, we work as one body; I may be without physical form, but I'm never without the full "body" of conscious awareness, knowledge, and interaction. Furthermore, I've slightly edited Antoine de Saint-Exupéry's words to further explain this concept: "Facing one another, we are love indeed but standing side by side and facing out to the world, we are a force to be reckoned with."

13. Thou Shalt, Thou Shalt Not

I think it would have been far more effective if Moses had brought down a disclaimer when he delivered those fateful tablets to the people of Israel.

- Thou Shalt not come to blows over these.
- Thou Shalt Not create divisiveness or a stumbling block.
- Thou Shalt Not worry yourself over every little detail.

As I mentioned earlier, these codes came at an earlier time in your history. They were necessary to help you define who you were and to distinguish your tasks as different from the apes', the cows', or the crows'. Nowadays they apply, but in a different sense. They exist to help redefine your focus.

Consider the words of the First Commandment: "Thou shalt have no other gods before thee." Take a moment to think about what is most often "before Thee." Is there a moment without your iPhone? While stuck in traffic, do you dream of having that car with the BMW logo? Or when you see a bird, do you automatically think of Twitter? Consider how universal the causes are you proclaim, the varieties of signs, or the alphabet that distinguishes NFL from ACLU or the Oscars from the Emmys. There are so many things that grab your attention; you must decide whether you're in or out or Brexit.

What that means, as far as the First Commandment goes, is that you already have so many gods before you that there's hardly any room for a Real God to show up. A golden calf that appeared eons ago is no match for the worship of today's *Golden Arches*. A real God doesn't want your money or your accolades. A real God sees who you are and only wants you to achieve your highest potential. You say those words as a kind of monotonous mantra. You talk about your mission or purpose, yet you have NO IDEA how important or how critical it really is for you to discover your true sacred mission and then align with it, get on with it, and give it legs to travel.

Although she felt our strong connection for a long time, Jo Ann never fully realized that part of her spiritual mission on earth would be to scribe this Gospel. She would constantly ask in prayer, "Jesus, why don't you speak out? We need your guidance now more than ever!"

And the whole time, I was both listening and speaking! But you see, if you complain too much about what is lacking in your life, you miss the opportunity to be the midwife bringing forth its opposite. So leave off challenging the Dos and Don'ts. Look instead to your complaints and protests. You may be surprised to discover hidden within them the magic formula that propels you forward and through to your Divine purpose.

14. Forgiveness

If you are having trouble forgiving others, then you are standing too far away from them. In fact, you have set up a barrier, a fence, or even a wall between yourself and the one you consider the *offender*. So now they have become the monster, and you are the *saint*. But recall when I admonished people to take the log out of their eye before they pointed at the splinter in other people's eyes.

It's so easy to see how flagrantly bad and wrong others are and to sit in your own seat of righteousness. This is the kind of obstruction I am talking about when I mention the log or mote in your eye. It's not a physical impediment but rather a limitation in how you actually see things. Suppose someone is swimming in the ocean. You only see the movement of the head and upper body; a good part of the lower body has been submerged by water and waves. Take this metaphor now to your wrongdoer. You only see the *upper body*—that is, the outer effect of their crime or their actions; you have not yet been able to submerge in the "waters" in order to see what is propelling them. Beneath the surface (were you truly to submerge), you would find pain, suffering, and ignorance, as well as a certain assurance that doing this particular act will relieve them (and the world) of the terrible suffering they experience. Can you find any type of accordance? Can your heart not be pierced by mercy or by grief at the prevalence of suffering and ignorance? And finally, standing very close and gazing into the eyes of the wrongdoer, can you not unearth some kind of forgiveness?

Those who find it hard to forgive have shut themselves off from the pain, which is universal and fills the heart not only of victims of violence but of perpetrators as well. Finding it hard to forgive others invariably winds down to finding difficulty forgiving oneself. Open the gate; take down the wall. Release the barrier. There is so much more to forgive in this world—both in ourselves and in one another.

You may remember when Peter asked me how often he should forgive the sins of his brother. I answered, not seven times but seventy-seven. What I really meant was that there is NO END to how much we can forgive, and every time we do so, we strip away the coverings, we remove the logs and motes and pretenses, and we come to rejoice in how we are one in the flesh and one in the spirit.

The Aramaic word for *forgive* literally means "to untie." In a certain way then, your hatred or negativity ties you to the person whom you can't forgive. Therefore, release and let go! Forgiveness is a great act of generosity. It helps loosen the ties that bind you!

15. Light

In every section of the Bible, you will find references to Light. In the beginning, Light is separated from darkness. In Isaiah, "people who walked in the darkness have seen a great light." John said, "Those who do what is true come to the light so that it may be clearly seen that their deeds have been done in God."

But what if I turned things around and said, "*You* are the Light of the world"? Whenever you let go of darkness, you light up the path with your brilliance. That's a good turnabout. You see, you've been thinking too much about visible light, such as sunlight or the light from your lamps and appliances or electric light. What you have yet to grasp is the amazing knowledge and spiritual sight that saturates waves and particles, arriving as the Energy promoting *Enlightenment*. That is not the kind of light you hide under a bushel or place on top of a nightstand.

That is the kind of Light that shakes you up and eventually wakes up the world. If you could travel at the speed of Light, you'd go even faster than 186,282 miles per second. (That is, of course, if Light obeys its own speed limit.) Your knowledge would be instantaneous. The tiny *gauze* covering your eyelids would vanish instantly, and you would see such brilliance shining in and through your Divine Self that you would immediately grasp that Light is what pours out from your eyes and kindles Loving connection, and Light is what pours into your heart and mind, offering glimpses of the true nature of Reality.

Light searches out the pathway for you, with or without your vision. I spoke frequently about those who came forward to be healed of their blindness and who, in the early stages, first saw men moving about like trees. When fully healed and with their vision restored, they realized that people finally came to look like real people. However, that was just the beginning. Until your inner vision is fully opened and until you access all the Light pouring in from the Universe, your perception of Reality is blurred, like trees walking around and searching their way back to wholeness.

16. Praise

It's interesting how many of the Psalms in the Old Testament are dotted with words of praise and thanksgiving (along with the predictable paragraphs of *woe*). From "Make a joyful noise" all the way to "Let everything that has breath praise the Lord," there is no mistaking the need to bring out all your cymbals, drums, and tambourines. However, if we harken back to Creation rhetoric, when the firmament was divided, night split off from day and the waters from Earth, and in that unique undertaking, God was inadvertently split off from humankind.

"As above" was not equivalent to "So below." God sat on the royal throne while humans, who were made of mud, had breath blown into them. It was not a great beginning. But if we revert to the spiritual principle "As above, so below; as without, so within," then we come to the inescapable conclusion of Oneness. "Serve the Lord with gladness" means we should honor the God and Goddess nature in every one of us. Love, joy, appreciation, and the clanging of cymbals are the birthright of every living being.

Nowadays, Positive Psychology will smile at you, offering the same message. It's not just that we owe praise and thanksgiving to God or one another, though certainly the lifting of ANYONE'S spirits these days is a great act of mercy and kindness. But remember that if our hearts are all connected and if we live energetically as One Body, then the offering of praise ultimately has a ricocheting effect. It bounces out to the Universe and bounds right back on a clear trajectory to your heart, lighting up your selfless offering of love and appreciation like a firecracker.

Praise is a heartfelt practice. It has a way of affirming life and strengthening the very qualities you deem worthy of praise. Without realizing it, there is so much more that you can give and increase in your own and others' lives simply by attending to what lights you up and what brings light to your comrades on the journey. As Paul might have said, reframing his own words, "Rejoice in Ourselves always, and again I say Rejoice!"

17. Prayer

Sometimes the disciples would get upset when I'd leave them in the middle of something important and go off to pray. Even in those times, the market would be crowded, the streets would be dusty, and people would be pouring in from other towns, almost as if P. T. Barnum was offering a new freak show, with sword-swallowers, bearded ladies, and this strange guy talking about loving your enemies.

At any rate, I needed to take respite. I needed to reestablish my connection with the Divine. Like everyone incarnated, we need occasional boosters or *reminders* of our connection. It's largely a matter of vibration. Think about the musical scale of Do-re-mi. You go from the lower *Do* all the way up to the next octave with the higher *Do*. Now all these notes are equal and necessary in the greater scheme of things. Imagine how symphonies would have turned out if you were only allowed to engage the higher *Do* but nothing from the lower register. Eventually, it would be monotonous and boring.

There is a difference though, when you consider the effect of vibration on our energy fields; we want to access those higher frequencies that help us be less earthbound and more expansive. We can match the frequencies of other energy systems, other stars, and even other galaxies. There, we *converse* with Light Beings of every stripe—those who truly are omniscient and who help us re-attune to our Divine nature. Remember, again, we are all connected through the basics of our Inner Being—Light frequencies, energy, intelligence, and the music of the spheres. We can dive into the vast pool of consciousness—the complex web of knowledge that exists in all parts of the universe at any time.

Here is a beautiful prayer adapted from the Tikkun Olam Chavurah and Fringes group from Philadelphia. It is called *Amidah: Seven Breath Prayer. Amidah* itself means "standing" and refers to the core group of prayers from the Jewish liturgy that are recited while standing:

> Breathing in I take breath into myself
> Breathing out, I join the web of being.
> Breathing in, I rest in the present
> Breathing out, I am past and future
> Breathing in, I honor the shrine of my body.
> Breathing out, I honor the shrine of the cosmos
> Breathing in, Presence fills me.
> Breathing out, Presence connects me to All Beings.
> Breathing in, I witness what is broken.
> Breathing out, I bow to what is perfect.
> Breathing in, I offer gratitude for what is.
> Breathing out, I accept that all things change.

Breathing in, I pray for peace for myself.
Breathing out, I pray for peace on Earth.

Prayer is an excellent medium. Meditation is an excellent medium. And though, in some ways, I may have pooh-poohed worship, that was because, in most types, you will find the underlying framework reflecting notions of Higher than/Lower than. After all, it's blasphemy for anyone other than the high priest to enter the Holy of Holies. Think of it. The preacher, in most congregations, usually sits on a raised platform; the rabbi, on the *bimah*. And you must be a certain age or a certain gender before you're even allowed a glimpse of many Scrolls or Scripture. Do you think that truly engenders a sense of equality? (Pun intended.)

Prayer, chanting, drums, silence, hymns, rosaries, dance, calling on the names of God, *Lectio Divina*, mantra, magic, foot washing, laying on of hands, anointing, Vision quests, fasting, davening, twirling, Praying Ceaselessly—these are wonderful accessories to the art of Divine Connection. Each one is designed to help us set aside our dual nature and attachment to Separation consciousness. When you leave off the encumbrance of comparison or judgment, you find yourself in a universe of peace, equality, and joyful Cocreation.

Many times, when speaking to the disciples or to gathered crowds, I entreated them to Pray and, often, to pray ceaselessly. Many took this to mean "Pray and you'll get what you want" or "Pray and your bad deeds will be forgotten." Although, at an elementary level, those things may in fact occur, the real reason to pray is *alignment*. When you pray, you align with me energetically; you align with all the potent forces of Light and benevolence in the Universe. You sense your connection is real; slowly, you recognize we are not that far away but *up close and personal*—indeed, totally linked. In addition, when you pray, by raising your vibration, you enter a new way of being. *Prayer* is just another word for evolution; with blended heart, mind, and compassion, you step into a higher path and way of being.

18. Divine Interaction

It is a powerful thing, at last, to wake up and realize that you and God have been having multiple conversations all along. You've been tuning in, receiving guidance, as well as the affirmation that this is a two-way street. We see you. We hear you. We know you in the totality of who you are.

At times, that can be a little distracting, even bothersome, for we may see divine parts of you that are even hidden from yourself, or other things you'd rather not see. Jo Ann often experiences this sense of "being caught" while having a hissy fit or eating too much sugar or cursing at her broken toilet. It's kind of like being caught with your pants down. Or better yet, it's like being caught with a flap of your heart wide open and the skin of your body removed so that we glimpse your internal organs. That's how naked *naked* feels. It would be insufferable unless you realize that our gaze is always sympathetic.

What we are connecting to is your Divine potential, which already lives side by side with us in the here and now. There is so much going on in the way of interactions that it is hard to describe accurately until you yourself wake up to the Reality. But in the meantime, trust that your prayers are heard and fully received—whether in the form of a plea, a praise, a confession, a wish, a sorrow, a gratitude, a request, or an apology. We are here with you in every kind of interaction, weeping or laughing with you, mumbling our own kind of thanks in your ear, and finding every imaginable way to be in dialogue and in Cocreation with you.

Now please step up to the Great Multidimensional Pantheon of Deities. Seat yourself and turn in all directions to receive a full welcome from your Brother and Sister Gods and Goddesses.

19. Confession

Long ago, the Israelites had a neat way of confessing their *sins*. They would tie multicolored ribbons or pieces of cloth to a goat and send him out into the wilderness. With such a ritual, they could be assured that their sins were fully expiated. Nowadays, you sit in little confessional boxes or off-load your woes with a psychiatrist. Frankly, I find the goat remedy far more effective.

For years, some people have been sitting, recounting, and rehashing the same experiences that got them into *trouble* in the first place. Although it may at times provide relief, more often than not, it keeps the same story and the same kind of participation in life active. Bless the helpers and listeners everywhere, and may you keep a drawer full of multicolored ribbons handy as a last resort!

In any event, there comes a time when your own personal history is no longer relevant to whom you've become. Would you wear the same dress you wore to your high school prom or the tie that went out of fashion when the Atlanta Braves won the pennant? I know I make this point several times, but it doesn't hurt to underline the fact that you keep changing and evolving. Yet somehow the way in which you represent yourself is different from what you've become. Think how absurd it would be to pump old blood into your veins (say, the blood you gave to the Red Cross fifteen years ago). It would no longer be a match. So why keep claiming the old story about life—your extremely refined, well-edited private tale of woe?

Oh, my people! My precious Ones! Once upon a time, I spoke to the poor souls of Jerusalem, telling them how much I wished to pick them up and fold them under my wings (as if I were a hen or a chicken). But the fox is absent from the henhouse now. You must go out into the world and find your new identity and encounter your Soul's wider landscape. Search. Create. You were meant to soar like eagles and not cluck around, pecking up bits of grain from the henhouse floor.

20. The Nature of Sin

For some time now, my dear editor has been asking about the nature of sin. This is no easy topic, and she has some fears about getting in the way or not expressing it fully (or heaven forbid—interjecting her own point of view). But that won't happen.

You can translate sin as "missing the target" or "being out of alignment." You can call it being mistaken. If you miss a step and tumble down the stairs, would you call that a sin? No, of course not. But I bring in that silly example because that's what humanity has done. We've put an overlay or judgment on making mistakes and, by that means, turned being off course into being wrong and sinful. I regret if, in my own way, I contributed to that through the lens of the Torah and so much comparison between good and not-so-good actions. I love what your Persian poet Rumi has to say about it; you could almost use it to update your awareness:

> Out beyond ideas of right-doing and wrongdoing, there is
> a field. I will meet you there.

Now I hear murmurs of panic and alarm. "What about rapists and murderers!" you cry out. Of course, they have erred, but there is a difference between erring and sinning. Things that harm others must be handled differently, but not with judgment, vilification, or condemnation. You will recall that when the poor woman was condemned for adultery, I said to the crowd, "Let whoever has not sinned be the first to cast a stone." I was utilizing the vocabulary of that time frame. We took actions very seriously and meted out punishment for everything small, medium, or large. Because we felt a greater need to control, avoid, or punish wrongdoing, we viewed it from the vantage point of separation consciousness, not unity or oneness.

But now in this New Age, there is an easier definition, much like the oath that physicians take: "First, do no harm." As we evolve in consciousness, we recognize the common ground among us—that we have all the same tendencies as a murderer but have not acted on them. We see the source of pain in the one who causes pain. So our perspective goes much deeper, and we come back to the underlying Reality of our deep connection in Spirit, one and all.

21. Unity

"Heenay ma'tov umanayim shevet achim gamyachad." Those often-quoted Hebrew words ("Behold how good it is for brethren to dwell together in unity") have been sung for ages. Although I quote an older version from the Bible, it is true that the other portion of humanity—shall we say, the *sistern*—has been entirely left out. It was a pity that, in those times, if one spoke about *men*, it was understood that women were included. It is a deluded, of course, and very handicapped point of view. Yet this is one more vestige of the Old Paradigm of Separation. It's as if our ancestors walked around with one eye covered with a patch and then proclaimed that the half of the world visible to them was the only aspect of Reality worth attending to.

Again, we must revert to the understanding that generations move through development and evolution just as individuals do. In today's world, there are three- and four-year-olds who grasp the mechanics of iPhones and can draw up videos or chats more quickly than their grandparents (and sometimes even their parents). Now whether this is actually a sign of evolution has yet to be argued. Taking a broader view, however, we begin to see the workings of progress, forward motion, and greater adaptation among humans, animals, and plant life throughout time.

Consider the organic development of life on earth. Take it down to the cellular level. When those first precious sperm and egg cells come together, have a *Meetup*, and declare themselves bonded, we have a sense of what to *expect* next. Before the full-fledged baby makes its appearance, however, there are hundreds and thousands of divisions taking place.

Cells pop up and split off to create a nose or a mouth, while other cells populate eyes, arms, toes, and so on. The first act in Creation resembles Division as much as Union, although naturally, cell multiplication is happening by the second. Meanwhile, cells keep waving goodbye to one another as they go about the business of colonizing different parts of the human body. And of course, we have seen the danger and difficulty of our various attempts to colonize the Earth.

I bring up this example to reiterate that key spiritual principle, which is "As above, so below." What takes place in the spiritual realms also shows up in denser form in matter. And so cells populate the body, while people populate the earth. It is part of a greater Expansion Project, which continues on into the spiritual realm. That precious Unity we seek depends on first creating the foundation from separateness. But eventually, that division no longer serves us. We must become whole. We must become One at Heart. When we finally climb out of our old separate turfs and territories, we can then remove the patch from our eyes and notice that we're all human and that we're all in this together— as opposed, say, to thinking of ourselves as African, Asian, Siberian, Semitic, or Seminole.

22. Parables

Sometimes you hear a much-repeated line, such as "A horse went into a bar," and then the inevitable response, "And the bartender asked, 'Why such a long face?'" and you laugh or groan. Jokes are a shorthand way of conveying information with a slight twist at the end. Although they're not *jokes* per se, parables also have a slight twist at the end or even in the middle. They're designed to topple some of your long-cherished beliefs, help you see the world in a new light, broaden your view of good works, or even consider who your neighbor may be, as in the Good Samaritan.

Parables were designed to contrast opposites—light and dark, rich and poor, barren and fertile—and, through comparison of dissimilar or strange things, help you up-level your consciousness. If you find a real treasure (in a teaching, for instance), you purchase the whole "field" to go with it. In other words, you help create an environment in which the treasure can grow, expand, and be shared with others. If, on the other hand, you arrive too late to meet the bridegroom (to whom you were betrothed), perhaps because you tarried or forgot to light your lamp, then you lose. You did not think of Union, got careless and unreliable, and when it might have been time for you to light the lamp of consciousness, you missed out. Never fear! Return again, for the light can easily be switched back on in your mind and heart.

It's not always clear what the parable is referring to, and that's the beauty of it (also the "beast"). If you wore the wrong clothes—meaning you did not honor what tradition called for or were somehow sloppy in your *appearance*, i.e., not showing up for the signal event properly "attired" with reverence and respect—then you were disinvited or thrown out of the wedding banquet.

So many little stories and vignettes are in the Bible, all with twists on their endings or unexpected events unfolding, all challenging your notions of goodness, justice, equality, mercy, loving-kindness, holiness, generosity, forgiveness, or acceptance. You understand that those symbols are placeholders for concepts you are leaning into but have not fully aligned with or accepted. When, for example, I told the fig tree not to produce figs any longer because it failed to yield just one when I was hungry, that was not an act of wanton destruction, although it may have appeared that way. On the contrary, I may have been modeling a new application of faith, but in this instance, having faith in your **own** Creative power.

If you imagine you can move mountains and have faith in your connection to the Source, then you surprise even yourself. You move mountains. What I am demonstrating is what we all hold in common, and that is our ability to cocreate with God. For instance, if the master gives each one of his servants money—one talent goes to one, two talents to the next, and five talents to the third—and then leaves, each has a choice in how to *spend* his wealth, which is a different way of saying *life force*. You go out into the world, play the game of life, and interact with others, and by your presence, energy is then doubled, tripled, or quadrupled. Or you can bury your talent in the earth, and no one benefits. Interesting, isn't it? How the word *talent* can be applied in the old sense, as well as with today's meaning. Recognize what precious gifts you have received from the Spirit and use them wisely, lighting up the world as you move forward.

The main problem in understanding the parables has to do with your own level of spiritual practice and insight. If you understand that the parables each held a key which unlocked a code or puzzle and that the true meaning would only be disclosed if you had attained that level of spiritual mastery, then you are better able to understand why the vignettes created so much perplexity and confusion. Why would anyone leave a flock of one hundred precious sheep only to search for the one who strayed? They might risk losing the ninety-nine others. If we're talking about actual sheep, of course, it makes no sense. If we're talking about care for humanity, then we must go out of our way to protect the innocent, the lost, or those who are on the fringes. Then turning inward to shed light on our own spiritual process, we recognize that all parts of us must also be "brought back into the fold." This message applies equally to the one and the many. But on a personal basis, we must engage in spiritual work to retrieve the *lost* parts of ourselves—those qualities we may have despised, denied, or denounced as unworthy— and accept and integrate them back into the wholeness, back into the oneness.

If you reread any of the parables, then look for clues to your own awakening and your own fulfillment, not so much in external things but rather in your Soul's inner calling to make peace with all parts of you and to connect more deeply with the Mystery of the Divine.

It is true that when I offered parables eons ago, I was often playing with the disciples. I used a lot of symbols. I also turned things sideways and upside down. You see, they were used to being very focused and serious about their business, and the parables had a way of waking them up, sideswiping, or shocking them into silence. Then they put on their thinking caps, trying to find ways to think out of the box.

Not all parables were transparent or even apparent, which was perplexing (and sometimes unnerving) to them. But that was how they received their training in Unity Consciousness. Consider this. There's always a place for Mystery in your life; not every answer you're dying to receive follows immediately on the heels of every question. Can you wait? Will you give the Parable a chance to gently unfold its meaning, like a newborn butterfly leaving the chrysalis?

23. Is Laughter Allowed?

Recently a pastor commented to members of his congregation that he was uncertain if laughter was permissible in Orthodox religious services. And of course, many people question the appropriateness of people clapping their hands if a musical piece has been well played or laughing out loud for any reason during the service. It may be hard for you to understand since not much humor got recorded in the early Gospels, but we actually did laugh from time to time—me and the disciples. And just like little children giggle in the back of churches, there were often snorts and snickering among ancient worshippers in the Temple.

There are some who may discount what is written here, because of the humor and lightness that is expressed at times. Again, that is too bad. It is the same as with scientists wanting verification that every single word is definitively true and irreplaceable. You will have a hard time doing that even in the strictest scientific circles. In regard to the Bible, for example, there are many who argue about which mountain Moses climbed eons ago and on which one I officiated. Was it Mount Sinai, Mount Horeb, or Mount Tabor? Was it a mountain in Saudi Arabia? Or was it even as far away as Mount Bucarest in France? Proof may one day be declared, but it's no substitute for what takes place with an actual shift in consciousness.

Laughter is a good remedy for the Soul. In any recipe, it creates "leavening" and sweetness. If you dismiss lightness of being and find it hard to laugh at yourself, you may have a hard time plodding through life. A poet once remarked that those who know how to laugh at themselves will always have a new reason to do so. However, if you think that laughter and truth do not mix or that humor cancels out the serious message of Scripture, then I suggest you stop reading right here.

At any rate, who said you had to be tight-lipped or buttoned up? I do not recall any commandment forbidding laughter in worship or in Scripture. One caveat that is to be mentioned, however, is that anything goes, so long as it's not offensive or harmful to anyone. Remember: first, do no harm. And of course, I myself am guilty of suggesting various penalties or punishments for wrong-hearted behavior. I once said, "If your right eye offends you, then pluck it out." If I have offended anyone in what I am saying, then I am deeply sorry, and I offer my apologies. I sincerely meant no harm. However, I confess it will be difficult for me to pay the "penalty" until I'm back on earth again.

24. Faith

Looking back and reviewing key Gospels, you will trip over the notion of Faith so many times you may begin to be inured to it, perhaps failing to notice that it's even there in the text. For perhaps one hundred times or maybe even five hundred times, I told people that their Faith had made them whole. Why is that so? Is it only the faithful who can receive healing and wholeness, like some kind of elite group? If you examine those who received healing, however, most folks were poor, blind, widowed, disabled, crazy, facing the death of a loved one, or in some way different from the average sheep in the flock. These were people who had suffered years with things that were considered incurable. We can say that they truly paid their dues. And at the same time, they were hungry—no, ravenous—for relief.

A great story from the yogic tradition illuminates this point, for there was a young man who sought out a sage in order to study with him and sit at his feet. Many people had spoken about this teacher, and so the lad was convinced he was the right one to approach. This was no ordinary teacher, however. He often took his students down and taught by the Narmada River in India. When the young man arrived and insisted that the teacher give him an audience, the sage merely smiled. "So you want to study with me. Is that it?" The *yes* was audible throughout the inner room. "Good. Let's have a little walk down to the river, and we'll see how it goes." When they immersed in the Narmada, the young man was surprised not only to be in waist-high water and soaked but also to discover that this sage was very strong and had suddenly grabbed him and held him under the water so he couldn't breathe. He kicked and fought, and just as his breath ran out, he was released. Sputtering and with a mouth and nose full of water, he yelled out, "Why did you do that to me!" But the sage was very calm. Peering at the young man, he replied, "When your desire to learn is as strong as your desire to breathe while underwater, then let's get back together and have a little talk."

In like manner, we need to have sincere *hunger* in order to enter the spiritual realm. Our faith grows stronger as we witness seemingly miraculous events or those we can appreciate are outside of our control. When we begin to truly *hunger* for righteousness, loving-kindness, or the fulfillment of our Soul's purpose, then we come up out of the water and breathe.

Of course, it's always possible to react—to resent, regret, or remonstrate against the evils of the world. But at every turn, life is offering you the possibility to strengthen your faith and participate fully in the Mystery. Not everyone will get out of the boat and walk on the water to meet me, as Peter did, but everyone sitting in the boat has the chance to witness miraculous events. The question is, what do you do with them?

How do you turn mystery into something translatable, into something acceptable in the language and currency of your day? Your faith not only makes you whole; your faith also gives you greater bandwidth with which to perceive the world around you. Then you can see there is so much more to you than this bag of bones. There is energy within you that contains Supreme Intelligence. Your faith creates an environment of welcome and acceptance—anything is possible. In fact, everything is possible.

I remember entreating the disciples to move mulberry trees with the very seeds of their Faith. As they witnessed my teaching and healing, they began to see a whole new way of being present to life (and life's suffering). They realized they needed to up-level their vision, their vibration, and their connection to the power and mystery of the life force within them. And that is exactly what happened. It continues happening to this day.

As your faith in the Universe grows and as you witness amazing things taking shape, you, too, are called into action. You, too, work with a greater palette and broader possibility. More and more, you find yourself willing to drop doubt and to trust in the magnanimous nature of Creation. The wealth of opportunities that arise and the responsiveness to need that you witness increasingly call out to you and induce you to take greater risks yourself. Why live in the Old Paradigm of doubt and confusion? There is a new World in the making.

Walking farther out on the limb, you trust that the tree will hold your weight. Or even before your arms start flailing about in the water and you panic as Peter did, you have a momentary flash of insight, and in that moment, there's no question about what to do. You rise to the occasion and step out of the boat, and for the briefest instant, you receive extraordinary feedback on the strength and resilience of your faith. There is no room for thought; faith shows up far in advance of cognitive thinking.

Deepening your faith, then, is like knocking on the doorway to Divinity. You achieve greater connection; you participate and draw to you miraculous events, and that very Energy of Faith calls more Faith to it and more to it. It's like muscles that get bigger and stronger the more you work out at the gym. The more you *work out* in the myriad faith settings around the world, the more your Faith grows, and then suddenly, inexplicably, you find yourself stepping out of the boat and walking across the water.

25. Ner Tomid

Light—flowing light. Everlasting light. Light is at the heart of our connection. Light runs through these pages. The Light in your eyes sparkles with the wisdom of your Soul.

John's Gospel mentions Light more than twenty times and reminds us to believe in the Light and become children of the Light. Yet it's not easy to accept that, at the core of our being, we are made of Light. After all, if you pinch yourself, you come up with a handful of skin, with muscle beneath, and beneath that, blood and bone. It's hard to imagine this human body reduced to such minuscule basic units—either wave or particle—that are essentially composed of Light.

If we are walking, talking, living, breathing bodies, how can we then be Light? It's no easy concept. But when you think of trying to walk in the dark and then flooding the room with light, you can picture it differently. With a simple light switch, it's easy to see where you're going. So it is with us all. As Beings of Light, we naturally and unequivocally point the way when we turn the Lights on within ourselves. But these are not light switches, nor are they the headlamps on your car. To truly light the way, you must turn inward, sensing the direction your Soul chose when it first incarnated. There was focus. There was a hidden purpose. There was an agreement you had made, and then you arrived. Life was not some accidental emergence or unplanned Earthly landing.

Ner Tomid is such a beautiful concept. It means "Eternal Light." It could be the flame that's burning in front of the ark where the Torah is stored. Or it could be the light that burned continuously at the Ancient Temple of Jerusalem. In any case, it reminds us that the Holy abides; the Holy is always present. And the most important Ner Tomid of all is the flame that burns continuously in your Soul, awakening at a cellular level the remembrance of your own precious Divinity.

26. Reprise on Sin

My dear Friends, it was necessary to provide some moral compass when, as a people, you were young and immature. Hence, we'll consider how this issue of sin might be applied today. Imagine how strongly you must get the message across so that your toddler does not run out into the street and get run over. Imagine how strongly you must convey to big brother not to swipe or hit little sister. Or imagine if a grown woman wants to kill her mother-in-law or a grown son wants to slay his dad. If you have not fully grasped the experience of *harm* then rules and regulations must be set in place. I agree that 613 of these codes, as you can find in Leviticus or Deuteronomy, are a bit excessive for our time. But one receives the external codes as a guidepost until they become internalized. When there is no more wish to conquer, maim, acquire, overrule, judge, possess, threaten, abuse, or act in a way that harms others, then the codes no longer belong to you. You belong to the codes and, as such, are free.

Of course, the Universal codes embodied in the Ten Commandments must still apply. However, you cannot receive the multiple and varied texts of the Old and New Testaments as the final stamp of approval or disapproval on your actions. It would be better to consider these testimonies as cautionary tales. Some of you dismiss them as irrelevant or mythological, and some abide by them as absolute authority. I see no problem with either approach, so long as the underlying theme—that of doing no harm—is not overlooked. If you are inwardly attuned to the three actions mentioned in Micah, to "do justice, love mercy and walk humbly with thy God," then you are on a good path. *Walk* can also mean "work," as in "serve humbly with thy God."

But that brings us full circle to this troubling aspect of sin. I will say this to you in all sincerity: I did not die in order to expiate your sins. I did not shed one drop of blood because of sin or evil, and more importantly, I did not die for you. I did not die to save anyone, because none of us need to be saved. We are already Divine, and we are already saved—all of us. We are in our Divine bodies and Divine location.

That does not mean there is no correction to the path, nor does it imply there is not more to learn. If you plant grapes in an arbor but the frame is crooked, then the grapes may grow sideways. Perhaps they grow in a way that is contrary to their nature, but in time, a correction occurs and the true path emerges. If you still cling to the idea of sin as an essential part of your nature, then think of sin as any action that separates you from the true Source of Life within you, from your Divinity—your God-Goddess-Angelic Origin—which is born with you into flesh and lives on with you as you transition from life and return to the Light.

I am not the only "God wrapped in flesh" you keep referring to. Can you grasp that you, too, are the Divine incarnate? When James and John argued about who would sit to my right or my left side, I had to laugh. Such a puny outing on the way to *heaven*! You talk about being one in the Body of Christ, but then you miss its true implication.

We're not up here sitting on either side of God, enjoying the view. We are in here—in our hearts—and we are side by side with you and with our own Divine Selves. I love how the Hindus portray Krishna dancing around the circle of Gopis, the lovely ladies. If you look closely, you'll see the same image of him replicated around the circle; in other words, Krishna is dancing with Gopi 1, Gopi 2, Gopi 5, 10, 10,000. That applies to each of us, only we are partnered within our own being with the Divine presence. Within us are the beautiful Radha and handsome Krishna, Lover and Beloved, throughout eternity.

You are both. Instead of Three in One, as you refer to me within the Trinity, take it down a notch and leave me out. Take it back to your own heart and soul. It's all there for you, and it's all there within you—Lover and Beloved, check; Divine Presence, check; and at One with All of Life, check. When you search deeply, you'll find the two in one within you, and the two and one always and only add up to One.

27. The Lord's Prayer

Thanks to Bobby McFerrin, Psalm 23 has been graciously reworded so that the presence of the female deity is recognized. There have also been a few variations to the Lord's Prayer since Mark and Matthew first jotted down the fateful words. I am grateful for all the upgrades. I am grateful also for the beautiful rendition of this prayer and other hymns that Mark Miller has arranged for our listening.

Regarding this seminal prayer, an important shift happened. It has to do with the word *Heaven*, which, before it alluded to the sky and stars, meant "that which covered things." It was only later that it came to be the place you inhabit after death or the place where only the good wind up. Interesting, isn't it, that we must line up in two different rows and move in two different directions in the Afterlife, based on our good or evil deeds? In the Old Paradigm, remember, everything worked in twos: either this or that, above or below, dark or light, good or bad. What if Noah had allowed three of each species on board the ark, or two old and three young ones? Surprise! Everyone goes through the same channel. As a Light Being, you simply drop everything within you that's heavier than the rays of Light and join the rest of us when life is over. By the way, we much prefer the word *Inter-Life* rather than *Afterlife*. It's less limiting. After all, you live many lives during, before, after, and in between the life you think you're actually living now.

At any rate, Heaven got a bad rap, once again causing a rift and playing up the good against the evil. It's the same with Satan, the "Avenger," who was really just an amazing challenger of ideas. He would have been a great lawyer if he had actually decided to incarnate. If anyone should sit on the Right hand of God, it's Satan. He deserves the honor because he was the Source of so many people's wake-up call.

Of course, we want everyone to receive their daily bread and not be led into temptation. But here's the thing: No God, Deity, or Angel worthy of the name would ever lead you into temptation. It's not in their province or their capability. But you ask then, "What about your forty days in the wilderness?" Oh, you mean my Vision Quest? Surely, Satan must have led you astray with so many tempting thoughts. Once again, we are back to duality, back to light and dark, night and day. "The animals came two by two." Then you might add, "And Satan met me on the dune, one more mountain to cross. He thought he'd lead me into ruin, one more mountain to cross."

Understand that when I'm playing with you, there is a method to my madness. The important thing to recognize is that back then, we didn't have the conceptual framework to portray an inner struggle; we hadn't yet received the concepts Freud brought in about id, ego, and superego. So the easiest thing was to break ourselves up into parts. The good one marches in to the tune of "When the Saints go marching in," and the bad one traipses out to the tune of "These boots are made for walking, and that's just what they'll do. One of these days, these boots are going to walk all over you."

Finally, the contest between Jesus and Satan was declared a draw. No one won; no one lost. It was the rise and fall of doubt versus discernment, and we all have our Forty Days in the Wilderness. That's because the work for each of us is to step up to the plate, discern what our true calling is, and then overcome the doubts and fears: What if I get too big for my britches? What if I can't rise to the challenge? Guess what. Your Forty Days are up, everyone. Come back to your beautiful life and learn to inhabit it fully.

28. Swaddling Clothes

I recently heard a sermon through the airwaves that has become my favorite; it was delivered by Pastor Brent Damrow at the First Congregational Church of Stockbridge. He spoke about how my mother wrapped me tightly and securely in swaddling clothes, and it was true that that process held me and contained me and helped me feel secure. It is also true, as he explained, that we need that sense of containment and safety if we are to truly thrive and grow. We need to know that we can be ourselves and be fully accepted as we are, no matter how it is that we show up. That is true for each of us.

But think how hard it is to truly extend that acceptance in all directions. Someone looks a little funny or can't talk the way you talk. Someone expresses different opinions, sports strange clothing, or wears their hair in a turban, a wig, or a do-rag. And immediately, your guard goes up. *Danger!* You think. *It is not safe to be with someone who is so different from me.*

That is a construct of the Old Paradigm that has passed its expiration date. The time has come instead to look more deeply and to see, beneath the clothes, the skin, and the language, a beating heart, a longing for love, life, and sustenance, which we all share in common.

I love Brent's metaphor of swaddling. But now take it a step farther. Feel in those supreme moments of stillness that you yourself are swaddled— that it is I wrapping my arms of love around you and that it is I loving, encouraging, protecting, and being the greatest champion for your stepping into the fullness of who you truly are. Now take that even a step farther. Remember that in our Divine Nature, we are not two but one. Then envision that you yourself are the Lover and the Beloved and that it is you who is holding on to yourself with such tenderness and compassion while, at the same time, it is you who is receiving the blessing of being held.

29. Reciprocity

One of the things everyone craves but often feels a dearth of is this sense of reciprocity—of give and take—as equals. It's more than mere give and take, which can often be translated as *quid pro quo* or barter and exchange. I give you a voice lesson, and you bake me a cake. It's not as simple as that.

Reciprocity has equality built into the equation. It also has the critical aspect of creating a match. You have been met fully in who you are and given back in kind. That is not always easy to come by. Why do you think we pray so often for a match *made in heaven*? Why do you seek psychics and fortune-tellers to let you know your soul mate is on her way? There's something deeper than mate and much closer to *soul* that's engaged in true reciprocity.

If recognition has anything to do with it, it's the sense of being mirrored—as if a mirror could reflect much more than your mere image. Beyond recognition is the idea of resonance; two souls resonate with one another, and the result is complete acceptance and vibrational equivalence.

If you asked me whether I experienced reciprocity in my former life, I would respond, "Absolutely." Using the words of the Lord's Prayer, which we prayed frequently in those times, I felt a constant support and energetic presence, in such a way that was mother and father, sister and brother, and friend and lover all combined. Imagine if someone could meet you at all levels of your being—climbing mountains or skateboarding with you, if that's what you love; playing chess or designing websites with you, if that's what you love; or arguing the fine points of the law with you, if that's what you love. You feel matched in your interests and, more importantly, *matched* in spirit. There is nothing else you need to do or say to know how deeply you are seen and appreciated. In fact, there is no love more miraculous and astonishing than that kind of love when it's reciprocated.

So how do you find reciprocity? The answer is, you can't. Find it, that is. You have to let it find you. However, you can position yourself to be closer on the receiving end by letting go of notions that it doesn't exist or that you're too old, too fat, or too unworthy to receive it. Through the gradual up-leveling of your thought and vibration, you actually *land* in a more spacious and susceptible reality. You begin to notice reciprocity among those whom you already know and love. Then you find yourself drawing more connections to you who appreciate aspects of your being—much more *like attracts like*. In a funny way, reciprocity occurs because you've given up on it and instead fallen more in love with your own life.

30. Tikkun Olam

There's not too much that can be said about taking care of the Earth that hasn't already been said, especially from those recognizing the need for strong countermeasures to climate change. More and more, the effects are visible, yet as a whole, humanity still seems to treat those changes as you would an Elephant sitting in the room that can largely be ignored.

In fact, the Elephant is a good metaphor. Carry it a bit further and imagine there's a whole stampede coming through your living room. After all, the Earth is your home. The Earth was a habitat specially designed for you and all other living things—plants, animals, minerals, trees, oceans, mountains. Everything was drawn into being as a perfect environment in which you could all thrive and flourish. But when you took dominion, things turned south. The original sense of dominion was for you to be stewards and caretakers of the Earth. But then, once again, we revisit the Power Over/Power Under dynamic of the Old Paradigm. You thought that protecting or caring for the Earth meant plundering or using it to your advantage, to the detriment of other species, to the spoilage of environment and resources, and eventually, to the tipping point—where the very life on Earth (and the life **of** Earth) is threatened.

Imagine the Earth as your home. Now take it a step further. Imagine what it would be like if you turned the very home you live in into a veritable pigsty. Every day, you would come home from work and tear up the carpets. Then you would trash the kitchen. In the morning, before leaving, you would rip open chairs and couches, and on weekends, you'd set fire to the upstairs bedrooms and destroy the garage. Soon your home (or what was left of it) would be uninhabitable. In the same way, the Earth is suffering from such abuse.

It's time now to wake up to this precious God-given land that was created in service to all living things. Clear the debris, put out the fires, and restore order, dignity, and the beauty of the original design so that life can recreate itself, so that life as we know can, in fact, survive. But first put out the fire in your own hearts that obfuscates your vision around stewardship or that has you feeling that anything in the environment is subservient to you and your wishes. As with all Living Beings, recognize that you and the Earth are equals and deserve to live on equal footing. Free the Elephant now from your living room and rejoice in the fact that, by doing so, you finally free yourself.

31. Eden

You will remember that at one point, I told the Scribes and Pharisees to render unto Caesar what was Caesar's and to render unto God what was hers. Up comes the idea of homage again. Whom do you pay homage to? Let your greater actions and involvements, your attachments and distractions provide the answer. Along with that comes the inevitable question: Do you share your wealth? Do you hoard it or render it or spend it wisely? In the New Paradigm upgrade, you can be wealthy or poor and still do God's work. But the question is, Can you do so one-pointedly and with heartfelt underlying intention?

The possibilities for service are endless in this world. It is not so much how many resources you have or do not have, as it is the quality of your intention and how you direct those resources. Are they filling your pockets and storerooms with items that will gather dust and last long after you're gone? Or are they bringing food, cheer, clothing, housing, instruction, support, and new life to those in need? The Old Paradigm said that there's not enough to go around, so hold on to what you've got. In the Paradigm of Love, however, we are ALL taken care of, and there's no need to be spurred on by thoughts of scarcity, fear, or competition.

It's a different mind-set altogether. In this sacred new Vision, you arrive fully grateful and fully delighted for your time on Earth. You trust in the capability of the Earth and all who have come before to pave the way for a fruitful and abundant life. You contribute to that as well. And you feel the togetherness of the setting; there's no sense of being alone or lonely.

No longer needing to be tossed out of Eden through a drop into Separation consciousness or the sense that you must fight for what you have, you feel relieved to discover you've landed there. Your life is a full immersion in that sacred Garden—abundant, rich, tasty, and endlessly providing for your needs. The serpent is easygoing and likeable, and you sense that this is a different Eden from the first one and that it has the potential to fulfill you beyond your wildest dreams.

32. Death and Resurrection

So why is there such a big fuss over my death and resurrection? Here is a place where history could really benefit from some alterations. Consider these notions: if you really want a king or a leader or a president to lead you, then you would risk losing your inner compass. But remember, as I spoke before, it takes time to develop that sense of inner compass. So instead, the shout for a leader becomes very strong. If we can't do it ourselves, let someone else do it.

"Lead us out of slavery! Lead us to a better place! Lead us on the path of righteousness! Lead us to the Promised Land!" Leaders can do that. But in those days, you were looking for someone to lead you away from Roman rule and Roman treachery. So you gave me your party's endorsement. However, I did not incarnate to lead you that way. I did not incarnate to lead a revolution, nor did I incarnate to start a new religion. I came to further my own Soul's evolution and to gather and cocreate with those of a similar vision. As often happens, people project onto would-be leaders every possible grace and every possible defect there is in the universe.

So you decided that if I let you down, it might be because I had a higher calling. If I wasn't going to lead you away from Rome, perhaps I was setting you on a path to safer ground. "Aha! Jesus is going to take us to Heaven. If only we are very good, nice children, then we get to ride with him." But you were mistaken. My Soul's evolution seemingly took me on a path toward death and destruction. I say "seemingly" because I did not die in the manner you envisioned. Instead, through my intensive training, coupled with that of my brother and sister pilgrims, I simply left my body on that cross like a disposable wrapper. As a group, we were playing with the art of regeneration.

Together we perfected the art of withdrawing consciousness from the body and propelling it out and back again into more favorable circumstances. It's important to recognize that this was no individual *savior* thing. In fact, if you want to cry "Savior," then you're better off alluding to the vast network of initiates and adepts who had been working this system for generations. It was they who indeed helped save me, and together we went on to continue the work of our Souls' Divine plan.

33. Let Go of Comparisons

You keep wanting to know why it happened **that** way two thousand years ago and why it's happening **this** way now. Why aren't there more correlations? Why did I speak words in a certain format that don't fit nowadays? How come Matthew talked about five thousand men gathered to eat loaves and fishes, but he only mentioned the women and children as an afterthought?

It was a different time. The emphasis was different. The focus of attention was caught up more in survival issues—better than, less than, who has the most strength? Even now, you have those who're climbing corporate ladders, treading on other people's heads. But the New Paradigm is emerging. There's less and less reason to go back and make sense or apply what happened before. Think about it. Can you go back in time, grab hold of the little knickers you wore at age three or the pretty pinafore at age four, and put them on now? Can you even remember what you were thinking about or how you explained life to yourself when you were ten? It was a younger version of you, and everything made perfect sense in that context but has less and less relevance to who you are now. That's because you keep creating the world in the way you see it and think about it. Isn't it time for an upgrade?

We keep searching for clues in history and science and exploration within the earth—in the oceans, out in the desert, or in the skies. Though it may be a contribution to humanity, there comes a time when looking backward no longer serves you. That's because you are, minute by minute and second by second, highly influenced by the focus of your attention. It carves out your place in the world. More importantly, it carves out your place within and the nature of your inner experience. Look then to the new future. Release the old stories of limitation—what you can and can't really do. Look instead to the possibilities you have yet to create. And consider this as we rewrite the course of history: together we are all growing and changing. I hope it doesn't surprise you to recognize that even your "Jesus" has evolved.

34. The Sacraments

Ever since my cousin John started dunking people in the waters of the Jordan, baptism has become one of the most important sacraments in churches around the world, whether orthodox or mainstream in their tradition. It's fascinating that baptism started out as a full-body experience. Come to think of it, plunging under that cold water may have provided a wake-up call of its own. Nowadays, you're lucky if you even have a few drops of water sprinkled on your head. But the idea is still the same: take this holy water and let it cleanse you of the past. In that moment's solemn ritual, you are no longer who you were; you are born again into a deeper relationship with the Holy, awakening into the knowledge of your own Divine Being.

According to their varying approaches, churches have defined sacraments in different ways. Sacraments cover a lot of turf—from birth to communion to marriage to illness or death. In some cases, they include the sacrament of being ordained or joining holy orders. Please notice that in each case, a sacrament points to a new chapter in life and a new way of being. You were single; now you're married. You were living; now life is ebbing away, and you receive the last rites to help you move into your "new life." You were alone, and with the sacrament of Communion, you take your seat at the Table of Love and partake of a heart-centered meal with members of your "extended family."

We could add a new sacrament that has not been alluded to before, although you've heard me speak of it often. We could mention the sacrament of Cocreation, a holy act of joining hearts, hands, minds, and spirit in working toward the common good, bringing your special brand of magic along with others to ignite these empowered acts of Creation. Look at Habitat for Humanity or the Red Cross or Doctors Without Borders for clearly defined Cocreative work.

There are many meanings woven into this idea of Sacrament, whose origin comes from the word *sacred*, and these can also include an oath, an allegiance, a ritual, or an act consecrated to the Holy. The main beauty of any sacrament—besides the fact that it calls us to be joined together (so, in a sense, all sacraments can be referred to as Communion)—is that a sacrament entails the embodiment of the Divine. We do not just think about a new venture; we are also engaged in it in body and mind. We are immersed. Bathed in the fullness of the holy water, we are encircled by the sacred fire; we place hands on the ailing body or feel the precious oil of our own anointing. In these ways, the body partakes of and joins with the Miraculous. Rather than telling the story in words, we enact it fully through Body and Soul, and somehow, by that means, the Sacred and the Mystery get fused together in our Being. Once again, we are made whole.

There is a beautiful Sufi song that originates in the Sikh Scripture in India. It presents this idea of embodiment, in which the One who loves God takes on the felt sense and spirit of the Divine as pure blessing.

> *My eyes are damp with the nectar of the Lord; my Soul is filled with her fragrance. Through Divine love, I am dyed a deep crimson, and this life of mine has been blessed. In the gaze of the Goddess, I am readily transformed. This body and mind are wet with the nectar of her Love. She tested my heart with her touchstone and found it to be pure. The song of Divine love is like a piercing arrow that has struck deep within my heart.*

35. Channels and Scribes

In the Old Testament version, a scribe was someone with a very serious occupation—that of copying down Scripture so it could be made more available. It was a great labor of love and exactitude. After Gutenberg, your scribes took a different turn. They started receiving "Scripture" in different forms and from Light Beings in Light. As a process, scribing is also channeling, but it can happen in song or poem, in the crafting of a painting or a symphony, or in the creation of architecture pleasing to the eye.

You may consider scribes and channels as weird and wacky people, but then you will have to consider yourself as weird and wacky too. For, you see, everyone scribes from time to time. Did you remember how to prepare that roast exactly like your grandmother did? Well, guess what, she was there in Spirit, reminding you of the correct seasonings. Did you worry that you couldn't put the vacuum cleaner back together after a few parts fell out? That was your mechanical granddad to the rescue. Even now Jo Ann keeps questioning how it is possible to be scribing continually via our connection. It is, however, a true cocreation in the sense that I bring in the Light, the Energy, and the encoded "Packets" of ideas, and then she uses her superior vocabulary and knowledge of Scripture to help decode and bring it into form.

Again, if you take the notion of Cocreation and combine it with the awareness that we are all continually and eternally connected in Spirit, then it's easy to understand how we work so well together in bringing forth new Creations (or improving on the old ones). It's too bad Genesis had Pop Jehovah as the only one breathing life into Adam or (in the alternate version) bringing Eve forth from a rib. This Creation project has been going on for centuries, and there's no way in h—— that it could be managed by one jolly old Soul. Shake hands with Divine Partnership and congratulate yourself on the fact that whenever you needed true inspiration, it came along at exactly the right moment.

36. Contemplation

Thomas Merton reminds us that contemplation is the highest expression of our spiritual lives. He said, "It is life itself, fully awake, fully active, and fully aware that it is alive. It is spontaneous awe at the sacredness of life."

How powerful it is to step aside from the continuous motion of your daily life experience, even for a moment. Most people regard stepping aside as actually stepping backward. "What? You mean I must forsake the sacred act of doing, accomplishing, competing, strategizing, succeeding, or moving forward? How will I survive?" It's a wonder to me that in the Twenty-First Century, people actually do survive without once looking back, sideways, or forward to take stock of their progress.

And by that, I mean their *Soul's* progress. How sad it is to wake up fifty years later and discover you were chasing your tail, or you were savagely pulling on the hairs of your head (to succeed) and wondering why you had such a terrible headache!

But now you can stop action. At any moment, take a few breaths. Look out the window. Sit on your porch or in the kitchen. Let go of all things electronic and close your eyes. Imagine emptiness for a few minutes. Now picture yourself at a crossroads. Looking down, you notice there are train tracks running parallel to where you're standing. In the distance, you can hear the whistling drone announcing the approach of the train. As it draws closer, chugging along, you stand at a safe distance, hoping to count the cars as you once may have done as a child. Now the sound is very loud. You watch as the engine and various cars pass by. One by one, they move quickly, with loud remarks against the uneven surface of the train tracks. As it is relentlessly moving forward, you may now feel as if you've entered a strange dream, hypnotized by the clatter of the cars moving along the track.

Suddenly you realize that while it's you who is standing by the train, it's also yourself that you notice sitting in each of the cars. You observe yourself when you were very young, peering out the window. Then you see later versions of yourself as an adolescent, as a young adult, then getting older, getting married, having children, and then approaching old age. Most of the time, you have been so absorbed inside the train, busily moving from one activity to the next and from one car to the next, that you don't even realize there's another version of you outside, looking on. You've stood and watched your own life pass by, and it happened in a matter of minutes.

Then abruptly, the train moves on. You see the caboose passing, and the vision is over. You realize then that you have hardly ever stopped to recollect the different aspects of your life, the momentary changes, the small "Ahas", and the great transformations. Yet all the while, you are growing and changing.

Contemplation is about stopping to take notice. It's about appreciating the insights and new beginnings. It's about releasing the old tired ways of being. It's a time-out, and it's also a time in. Sitting and breathing, sitting and watching, you begin to notice that you are not your life. Neither are you the thoughts you have about your life. You are not the story you declared and kept repeating to yourself as you moved from car to car within life's train. You see yourself living each day as you move from car to car, and in one exhilarating moment, you discover yourself to be none other than the Witness. You have the distance, the neutrality, and the compassion that come from stepping aside, standing outside the relentless passage of events to enter supreme Stillness. From that vantage point, you can observe your whole life with the true neutrality expected of a witness of events.

Then you come to that moment of exultation. You are not who you *said* you are. You are not living either in the train or on the road but in a state of Divine Grace. You are Creator Being. You are Divine. You have achieved what Merton calls the true *Contemplation*—having gratitude for life and for being. You awake to the "vivid realization that life and being proceed from an invisible, transcendent, and infinitely abundant Source." Contemplation is, above all, awareness of that Reality and of our ongoing connection to that Source.

37. The Cross

Walk into a church or a chapel, and what's the first thing that accosts your eye? Me hanging with my head tilted to one side, nailed to the cross. What a sad focus of attention! It amazes me that you even have hymns about the cross and that you deify the wooden contraption almost as much as you deify me. Those two pieces of wood wound up being a death trap and an ignoble exit from this world.

How is it that the cross came to have so much meaning and even preempted the more vital aspects of my ministry or the living reminders? You could have put me in a manger on the chancel or near the Communion table, dressed in my finest swaddling clothes, but instead you keep on reminding yourselves how terrible my death was (a death, by the way, which literally took about four full minutes). So much more time was spent in my actual landing here on earth, and yet the Old Paradigm begged for the difficult, the struggling, and the suffering aspects of life on earth, to reinforce and perhaps even remind you: "You do that thing you want to do, and soon you'll be hanging there beside him."

But all along, that emblem keeps reminding us of death. Death is on its way. Death is the supreme punishment. Two thousand years of having our minds be consumed with death when so much life was happening! Of course, I understand how that process came about; after all, I witnessed it in entirety and continued to be engaged in events long after I was gone from the Earthly plane. Since, as people, we are meaning makers, we must make meaning out of all events, even when the truth eludes us. As I said to you earlier, I did not die for anyone; I did not view it as a tragic or terrible ending. I knew what was in store. My cohort and I had been planning for that transition literally for ages. Now I'm not saying death on a cross is an easy or likeable thing, but since it happens swiftly and since you can remove your conscious awareness from your body in advance of the event, it's almost as if the folks watching suffer more than the ones who must die in that way. Nevertheless, I wish we could invent a new emblem for this life of Jesus. If you must stick with wood, then I'd like to put in a request to take out the cross and replace it with a Christmas tree.

38. The Path to Inner Freedom

What does it mean to be free? Consider how hungry the Jews were to be freed from Egyptian rule—so hungry that they abandoned regular meals and a regular routine in order to release the yoke and oppression of Egyptian rule. But if you follow their next set of adventures, you will understand that they soon became disillusioned with this *freedom*. There was no evidence of three squares and a bed in all their wilderness travel. Some even dreamed of being restored to captivity. The real question to ponder then is, What truly subjugates you? There are actually instances where a homeless man is inwardly freer than the chairman of a multinational corporation. So where is your fealty? Whom do you pledge allegiance to on a daily basis?

The experience of inner freedom is unique and unparalleled. It cannot be purchased for any amount of money. It is the side effect of multiple *tours* along your evolutionary route to wholeness. Just as with the Israelites, you taste the contrast, once having been enslaved and now having been freed. When no longer bound by empires, colonizers, or corporate raiders, you discover a host of masters to whom you pay your dues. Remember when I said that you couldn't serve two masters? Although it was based on the idea of external works and allegiance, the underlying intent was to ask what your heart was set on. What was your main focus? With that, we return to the idea that where your heart is, there your treasure will be and vice versa. For your heart and your treasure are inextricably bound. Can you sense who rules? Just have a look at the better part of your daily activities, your weekly routine, or your monthly set of goals. What you see in that configuration is the outline of your heart's focus and the perceived *treasure* beneath it all.

Inner freedom comes at the end of so many enslavements and addictions. It's the unwrapping and unwinding of lifetimes of tendencies pulling you outward and away from yourself. Finally, there's a lull in the movement of the tide rushing out to sea. For a moment, everything is calm. Then the inevitable takes place—the water rushes back to shore just as your inner hopes and wishes change direction.

If you read the preacher's lament in *Ecclesiastes,* you know his conclusion: all is vanity. His sorrow and dejection at the things of this world form the perfect springboard for returning to the Self. Return to the cultivation of one's inner knowing, one's indefatigable treasure that lies within. If you read the first chapter of the *Bhagavad Gita,* likewise, you will find in Arjuna's dejection and in his refusal to enter battle that same pause between the outrushing and the inrushing of the sea. It formed a distinct line of demarcation. At last, you discover that everything you ever wanted, chased, explored, pursued, or yearned for eventually led to the experience of emptiness. This is not what it seemed. This in fact resembles the preacher's cry that we're out here chasing the wind. Despite having slid into the emptiness of most life pursuits, it doesn't mean that you stop pursuing. It's just a turnabout point. It's the moment in which you are reminded of the vanity of external movement when the true and only fulfillment winds up being chiefly an internal development. You may well focus outward (and indeed the world needs it); however, you extend from the place of the inner lining—from the very depths of your Soul.

It is that hungering to be in alignment with your Soul and your Soul purpose that wakes up latent hungers and fuels endless inner quests. Your prophets and poets have spoken of this for ages. Shakespeare mouthed the words "To thine own Self be true," which could conceivably have *shaken* us out of our oblivion centuries ago. But it is no easy thing to wake up. You hear the alarm ring, then you engage the snooze button. How much simpler would it be just to go back to sleep? However, the call to inner freedom is more persistent than your alarm clock. It wakes you up at dawn and in the middle of the night. It will drag you out of the wedding feast or the office party. "Time is up," your Soul calls out to you. Your *time-out* is over. Now is the time to focus inward. Throw off the covers. Get out of bed and open the curtains. When you notice how much light is pouring in from the sun, recognize that it's no match at all for the billion-kilowatt hours your Soul manifests as you explore its inner dimensions and as you reel from its overwhelming brilliance.

39. Grace

Many times, you have heard how grace is a gift that is unearned, undeserved, and unmerited. If you could know the Divine Reality, if you could live just a moment in our shoeless shoes, then you would know how much you are loved and cherished for who you are. You might also be surprised to learn that we follow your progress very closely in your life on Earth, shedding Light on your direction and crowning you with Love and Grace.

Those of us in Spirit are much more attentive to you than you are to us, but that is not meant as criticism. On the contrary, it has to do with our different roles and appointments and our different locations and time usage. By now, you are aware that Light Beings in Light operate in a timeless zone. We can see the interconnectivity of all your lives and all our lives, whether in Spirit or incarnate. Abraham, the channeled Light Being who comes through Esther Hicks, often reminds you that you are "out here on the leading edge." If you picture life as partnering in a huge global theater, then you are the ones on the stage, while we have fun reminding you of your lines, shining spotlights here and there, and occasionally raising or lowering the curtain. But it's always a cocreated event, and each of us have our preassigned roles.

Being on the Leading Edge, however, puts you front and center on Life's stage, testing out the very principles you study so assiduously when you are between roles or, shall we say, between lives. So grace is an event that reminds you how kindly you are held, how much you are appreciated (no matter how you show up), and how much we champion your every move. From time to time, something unexpected shows up in your life—something you had hoped for or something you didn't even realize was your heart's desire. Then it seems like a miracle or perhaps a mirage. But when you look closely, you see that it's a clear sign from the Universe. We are in this together. Your desires are known. You are loved. You are graced in this life on Earth. We have your back. With that, you can relax. Appreciate how extensive your partnering with Beings of Light is. In fact, you do not have to work so hard to receive God's approval. You do not have to search or pray for grace. To paraphrase Renée Zellweger's great line, "You had it at 'hello'!"

40. Open and Affirming

You have no idea how astonished I was to discover that in your churches nowadays, you put this question to a vote! First, you had to decide whether to admit people of color, then different nationalities, and now you're questioning whether to accept folks who are gay, straight, bisexual, or transgender. Really? I had hoped by now you would have released the Old Paradigm judgments and distinctions about color, clothing, what folks wear on their heads, or their preferred choice of organ between their legs. Is it really a wonder that wars and crime persist? When will you get over your addiction to hatred?

It's sometimes hard for us Light Beings in Light to observe you, who, despite being Light Beings incarnate, still harbor so much blindness and negativity in relation to others. Yet these are vestigial remains, the signs of old Paradigm effects wearing off and gently fading into oblivion. As I've said earlier, it's time to focus on the Divinity in everyone you see that can help you accept the humanity in all and the fact that if you look closely, most people actually have one heart, two eyes, one mouth, two arms, one anus, and you get the rest of the drill. Of course, there are occasional exceptions.

But consider in real terms, What harm may come to you if someone chooses a different sexual identity from the one they were born with or a different partner or a different style in bed? Does it really interfere with your lifestyle? If you answer yes to this question, then it's clear you need to juice up your own sexual activity.

Likewise, I regret the emphasis of the old texts, which created so much confusion about sodomy, bigamy, women's sovereign right to their own bodies, enslavement, and other variations on the Power-over/Power-under theme. If I were able to excise all those texts, naturally I would. But if you simply gaze through the lens of Twenty-First-Century equality, wisdom, and compassion, you will finally understand that there is a place for every being and for every being's personal choices (so long as no harm comes to another) and that each one has sovereignty over their physical and mental well-being, their gender, their choice of partners, and their own life and Soul expression. How can anything less work for humanity in this Age? If you exclude even one of these, My precious children, then you exclude me as well.

41. Transfiguration

You may have heard about what happened to Moses when he went up on Mount Sinai to receive the Ten Commandments. In that magical event, he was deeply moved, his face lit up, and his energy was completely transformed. In order not to blind his people, he had to wear a little veil over his face after he descended.

In the presence of so many high-octane beings, you are filled with so much light that there is a danger your electrical system will shut down. Thus, a circuit breaker is included. That sometimes includes a shift into deep sleep, sometimes passing out and (very infrequently) passing on. So I was not the first to ascend the mountain. However, the difference was that I did not go alone. I was accompanied by Peter, James, and John, who, when they first laid eyes on Moses and Elijah, wanted to immediately set up camp. It was very sweet of them to care for us in that way; however, Moses and Elijah had already reserved accommodations elsewhere.

What was transfigured? A few thousand (or perhaps even a million) cells in my body. I was again reminded of my Sacred Mission and felt a renewal of faith, strength, and conviction. What you may not have realized, however, was the fact that Peter, James, and John were also transfigured, although without the glowing faces or the white robes. Remember that they slept afterward. It was during that time that they were visited by Divine energies; it was at that time that much of their visionary heart and healing activities were raised a few octaves.

It's too bad none of the Gospel writers interviewed them immediately afterward, although Luke recorded as best as he could what transpired both in his Gospel and in Acts later on. Now think of other instances when disciples happened to be sleeping, and recognize that it's not just avoidance or ducking out of the frame. Instead, it's part of Divine Expansion and the transformational work of Spirit.

You see, each of us has the ability to be transfigured. We all have access to the highest frequencies and the most profound states of consciousness. In a way, the Mountain is just a symbol for the alchemical process that takes place and the fact that you go up energetically but not geographically in expanded awareness. Many spiritual and consciousness-raising events have been described that way in the Bible so that the masses can get a better grasp of the process. After all, there are so many who are tuned in. There are so many who are on the cusp of transformation!

42. Peace

Pacem, shalom, *paix, paz*, salaam, *taihei, wa*, pax, *shanti*, peace—Peace be with you. Peace on earth. How interesting that the Japanese have more than fifteen words for peace. How many can you conjure in your native language? It tells us something about how earnest each of us is in the pursuit of peace. The peace of Christ be with you. The peace of Isis be with you. The peace of Shekhinah; of Muhammad; of Thoth and Seshat; of Kwan Yin and Buddha; of Saraswati and Vishnu; of Ra, Raet, Ma'at, and Nefertiti; of Parvati and Mahesh; of Pachamama and Pachakuti; of the Peruvian Shamanic tradition; and of the White Buffalo Calf Woman. With so many beautiful traditions and so many Light Beings to remind you of your path and light you up with the brightness of the Stars in the Firmament, how can you *not* yearn for peace?

Think of this notion of Peace: Suppose you had to go back and list its antecedents in Scripture. Then you'd rifle back at least fourteen generations to discover when it first appeared. You'd find a lot of "begets" and "begots" but only a rare allusion to peace. Then travel back another fourteen generations, and on and on. Where do you find the beginning of peace? Where do you locate its middle? Or have you already written it off as impossible?

The Third Chinese Patriarch, Seng-Ts'an, had some powerful words to help us understand peace. He said that if you wish to know the truth, "then hold no opinions for or against anything. To set up what you like against what you dislike is the disease of the mind." Hold no opinions! And then, to give us further insight into peace, he said:

> When the fundamental nature of things is not recognized
> The mind's essential peace is disturbed to no avail.
> The Way is perfect as vast space is perfect,
> Where nothing is lacking, and nothing is in excess.

Consider that peace takes up its origin and its home in the center of your heart, where all things sacred are birthed; it emanates from your smile to your speech to your handshake to your openhearted hug. It is the peace that's shared in a hundred different versions in a church or synagogue or mosque or shrine. But more than a word or a handshake, peace is a force that animates all life. A bright, shining beacon, you are Peace in the world when you have at last waved the white flag signaling truce and have declared all war null and void within your heart.

43. Being Present

Nowadays, there is so much discussion about being present that you could almost nickname the Twenty-First Century the time when folks decided they had actually *become present* to reality. It is the buzzword for every kind of activity. Can you be present while you eat? Can you be present while you work? What keeps you from being present when you meditate?

The ability to be present is actually what distinguishes most of your endeavors from being commonplace (or automatic) versus being fully attended to and thus fully experienced. I love how Eckhart Tolle equated presence with holiness when he said, "The moment you enter the NOW with your attention, you realize that life is sacred." That is because you notice the theme and the underlying energy of events—the interconnections and small surprises. You grasp your role as Creator. (In another little surprise, one of the translations for the Hebrew word *God* actually means "The One who is always *present*.") So intermingled with the Divine, you have a chance to witness and be continuously present. Gradually, you become aware of the special connection between heart, mind, and life experiences, reminding you again of this amazing feat of Cocreation in Spirit.

To be fully present, however, means giving up the Old Paradigm's view of struggle. To accept and to be fully present for experience in many ways are equivalent. That's because when you move into acceptance, you access a more merciful, broader perspective from which to view things, and you dive deeper into the core of experience and the core of our interrelatedness. To be present is to exist within the unity and wholeness of life rather than splitting off in any particular direction. When you no longer do that, then you are fortunate in no longer having to experience divisiveness or the splitting apart of your own precious life force.

44. By Whose Authority?

You will remember during my ministry that there were many people who were uncomfortable in my presence, questioning what right I had to teach or by what authority I was preaching. After all, I didn't have a Doctor of Divinity, a license, or a rabbinic or priestly degree. Yet I spoke with confidence, clarity, and truth, knowing I was channeling the tenets of the Divine. I was the conduit or the vessel. In that process, there could be no corruption of the truth. Yet during one of the high-profile recorded encounters about my authority, I was accosted by the Scribes and Pharisees of the Temple, who were beginning to fear that I might replace them or agitate the people or disrupt the status quo. So they asked me point-blank: "By whose authority do you speak?"

Remember how I responded? I asked them if the baptism performed by John the Baptist in the River Jordan was authorized by God or by man. This stopped them in their tracks. Reasoning that with either response they'd get caught (or rather, that they'd catch themselves), they backed out and said they didn't know. I responded that, in that case, they wouldn't be able to *know* the Source of my authority either.

It is not easy to hear godly language or words of wisdom from an unknown source. We gravitate to our rabbis, our priests, our Imams, our bishops, or our Lords to find out what Divine life is about, as if you needed a special license to access the Holy of Holies. In the New Paradigm, however, at any given time any one of you can be the mouthpiece for God. In fact, it's much better if the task is widespread, so that we can all hear the message through different lenses, languages, and interpretations. Imagine if only one Gospel had survived!

You see, you have taken Scripture too literally. Instead of viewing it as a building block or foundation from which to live your life, you've managed to turn it into a closed airtight structure, which, year after year, gets older and moldier, not only admitting no air but also no new Light on the subject. That is a good recipe for entropy.

On the contrary, Scripture needs to change and evolve just as you do. It needs to stay current with who you are and with what your evolving level of consciousness requires. That is why, at different times, I and other Light Beings feel compelled to come through and align in thought with those ready to receive and disseminate the message. Little by little, its vibration is then channeled upward a few octaves.

It is good for you to come face-to-face with renewal, with your inner knowledge refined and rekindled in the Light of Spirit. Resurrection was not meant to only apply to the body or to the aftermath of physical death. Instead, we are each of us resurrecting a new *body* of wisdom, day by day, increasing our perspective, our knowing, and our way of being, which literally penetrates down to the cellular level.

It is also good to read and connect with an updated version of Scripture, and this is not the only one. Many Gospels have escaped your notice. But now that you are entraining with a new reality, soon you, too, will have the same fervor and perspective, connecting to a vision that lights you up and enables you to add your own updated version. Take this on. As much as I've spoken about Cocreation, did you think Scripture would be left out of it?

Relax. Let go. As Julian of Norwich used to say, "All is well, and all manner of things are well." And in truth, all things are working toward their highest good. There is no need to hold tightly to any tradition or idea that has passed its term of usefulness. Remember when I said that "man wasn't made for the Sabbath; the Sabbath was made for man (or woman)"? Well, the same is true of these teachings. Humans were not made to conform to Scripture; on the contrary, Scripture was created in service to humanity. It cannot serve you if it is not a match for who you are or who you're becoming as you move through the stages of your Soul's evolution.

Stop. Take a breath. Know that there are more precious holy moments in life than you can ever capture, count, or record. So relax. Your life itself is a Scripture.

45. Covenant

By now, you are catching on. There is really only one Covenant you take on in any lifetime, and that is the choice to be in alignment, to be in agreement with and in Cocreation with the highest good—in essence, to take on the work and remembrance of yourself as God. But then the puzzling question must appear: Which God are we talking about? Are we talking about the God who stomped through the Garden of Eden or moved above the ark in a great pillar of smoke? Is it the God who spoke among the leaves of the burning bush or the God who thundered and rained down floods on the Earth?

Which is your God of choice? There are so many to choose from: You can offer incense to Zeus (and avoid his thunderbolt), or you can pray to Allah or chant to Kali, who has a necklace made of skulls wrapped around her neck. You can look to the Underworld Gods or those inhabiting oceans and waterways or even pray to Parvati, who stood on one leg for ten thousand years as her great spiritual sacrifice. Eventually, however, you must come back to consider that overarching commandment: "Thou Shalt have no other Gods before thee."

As long as humanity has believed that God could be pinpointed either in form or formlessness, there's always been a mix-up, a kind of spiritual traffic jam. The commandment would have saved everyone a lot of trouble and avoided a lot of bloodshed if instead it said, "Thou Shalt have only One God *within* Thee."

Which, of course, is stating the obvious. Recognize, however, that you are and always have been in covenant with the Spirit. You and the Divine are inseparable. Just as you go through life and receive many names—you could have a childhood moniker; a nickname; a teenage play on words; a first, middle, and last name; and then possibly a married name or a doctor or doctorate in your name—so too have you given out all these names and appearances to God when one and only one would have sufficed.

Can you look in the mirror now and see that unchanging face of yours beneath all the changing faces and appearances? If you gaze for a long period and let your vision cloud over, you may get a glimpse of your unparalleled and eternal Divine features.

46. Judas and Mary Magdalene

Who would have imagined two more unlike people being lumped together in this part of the narrative? Despite their obvious differences, however, it was both Judas and Mary Magdalene who shared a trait in common: each, in their own way, was absolutely fearless; each grasped the nature of our Sacred mission on Earth and were willing participants; and each was accustomed to thinking outside the box.

It was not a case of either/or—either Judas was a betrayer or not, either Mary was a lustful sinner or not—as your history seems to proclaim. It was both/and. Everything they were and all aspects of who they had been were necessary elements to bring to the table. As I've said before, it is rare for a person to live only one life while alive; most have one, two, or even three incarnations while still in human form. So it was with Mary and Judas. Judas's cunning, his activism, and his heart that burned on behalf of the needy and the poor were what positioned him to do the deed, as it were. But as a Light being, he saw the plan and saw how we each played a role. He was and is very dear to me, and just as you have relegated Satan to his infernal position, it will be good to stop demonizing Judas as well. He had his specific directions.

Mary Magdalene, on the other hand, was the disciple who most understood my mission, not from her head but from her heart. Subservient to men in a prior experience, she had nevertheless learned a great deal from men; she knew how to read their intentions and could spot danger or delight instantly. On her own, she begged me to change direction, because she *saw* the whole enactment long before it came to pass. I call it enactment because in many ways, it did resemble the kind of Passion Plays that you keep repeating through the ages. But while Mary saw events way in advance of their unfolding, she also had the kindest and most moldable heart and mind. Through her life, she had truly learned the art of surrender. It is different from what you might imagine.

True surrender comes with equal parts of deep, abiding love and long-suffering pain. True surrender is the highest act of Faith. Mary may have long ago surrendered her body to the whims of man, but this final surrender far surpassed anything she had ever known. And the same was true for Judas. Imagine being an accomplice in the delivery of your precious Loved one into the hands of so-called Justice, as Judas was called to do. Then imagine the torturous events of witnessing his demise, as Mary Magdalene had done, even knowing that he was safe and protected (despite all evidence to the contrary). More than any other disciple, Mary Magdalene understood what the profound process of letting go in body and surrendering oneself up in Spirit amounted to.

The Bible depicts her as the chief presence postmortem; however, the truth is that many of my closest disciples were there on the *watch* and present afterward to help me achieve the necessary healing and care that would help me transcend and then emerge in my fully resurrected Divine body. It was an event we had rehearsed and prepared for long before it occurred. If you did not receive news of it in the Gospels, it was because it had been withheld as part of a secret tradition long observed through the earliest Mystery Schools on Earth.

Now you have a new way of perceiving what occurred more than two thousand years ago. Instead of being a one-person sacrifice then, Resurrection can be seen as a group endeavor. You may still look upon it as sacrifice, and there are some unpleasant moments, of course. However, when you agree to an assignment in Spirit that you know will awaken everyone's understanding of Life, Death, and Return to Life, then you surmount the difficulties because you are in total Covenant and total agreement, absolutely aligned with the outcome. That outcome has been slow in emerging, from the perspective of Earth time, but in other dimensions, it is occurring at the Speed of Light.

47. Travel Insurance

In Ancient Israel, we traveled by donkey, colt, or caravan, and frequently on foot. We were a peripatetic people; wandering was in our nature. After all, it had taken more than forty years to arrive at our destination. There was no way to ensure safe travel, despite all our wanderings. We had no policies or travel insurance available. Donkeys or people often lost their footing; roads were not macadam, and thieves used the cover of darkness to surprise nighttime travelers. Our only insurance was placing our faith in God and (as the saying goes) securing our camel or donkey.

Now a journey of twelve hours by road can be handled in a two- or three-hour plane flight. You can trot around the globe meeting people you would have never even known existed five hundred or six hundred years ago. Whether you travel by land, air, or sea, today's journey takes place in an altogether new dimension though. It is the search for Union that has you traveling uncharted distances, entering unknown realms and arriving—where else?—at the center of your heart. You might say, "Well, that's a short distance." But it's a heck of a lot longer than the measured foot or so from your head to your heart.

This is a brainy culture, above all. You may be surprised to learn, however, that it's your heart, not your brain, that is the portal to new and unknown worlds. It's your heart that helps you travel to other dimensions—all part of your Soul's access, feeding an expanded awareness of who you are and what you are capable of. If you are a true spiritual pilgrim, then this journey within has endless destinations. It could be other lives or other time frames; it could be roles you've played that are now coming back into prominence or identities that occur as obstacles you are now seeking to dispel.

If you could see yourself as we see you, you would know the extraordinary reach of your physical, mental, emotional, and energetic configurations. You would see how far out you've extended, how many worlds you've inhabited, and how great your contribution to the evolution of consciousness everywhere is.

If you can move from a donkey to a jet plane, that represents a mere trifling change in travel. Instead, allow the presence of so many Light Beings in Light to remind you that you have excellent travel *assurance*— in other words, the option for Instantaneous Pilgrimage. It's something you won't be able to find on your passport, but your right of passage is always guaranteed.

48. Back Home

After all our travels in different directions through different landscapes and lifetimes, the beauty of a Soul Pilgrimage is how it brings you back home utterly transformed. Look around your home or apartment. Notice the china, the lamps, the fold of curtains, or the way books are stacked on the table. You've come back home, and although externally everything looks the same, internally your world is upside down. You have changed. Your thoughts are not the same. Your body is lit up from within. Your awareness continuously grows brighter; instead of a dimmer switch in the living room, you seem to now have a *brightener switch* installed within the cells of your body that just keeps getting brighter, glowing with the daily increase in awareness and love. While you may feel your pain more acutely, you also feel the easy abandonment to joy and ecstasy increasing. In brief instances, when old patterns resurface, you find it easy to renew your faith and not dwell on diminishment of any sort.

All your travels have brought you home to your True Self and, simultaneously, to the inner family that welcomes you with open arms. It's as if you yourself embody the father, the Prodigal Son, and his older brother outlined in Luke's Gospel, all wrapped up in one. One part of you took off for a while, one remained with resistance, and meanwhile, Dad opened his arms wide, overjoyed to have everyone reunited. They're all part of you within you.

You may have left home a thousand times, but here in your deepest heart, you can always be found. Now sit on the sofa or your very best chair. Put your feet up and get comfortable. Acknowledge that your pilgrimage has brought you to the most Sacred site of all—that is, your heart—then with great joy and applause, welcome yourself Back Home.

49. On Love and Holiness

Paul spoke some of the most beautiful words in your Bible when in Romans, he proclaimed that "neither death nor life, nor angels nor principalities, nor powers nor things present, nor things to come, nor height, nor depth, nor any other creature, shall be able to separate us from the love of God [period]."

Now of course, he singled me out as the one container or conveyor of that love, and it was very kind and reverential of him. Yet as we're approaching completion of this Twenty-First-Century Gospel, you have received a greater view and a deeper understanding of Love and Holiness. You can see that Love (if worthy of being called Love) can never be confined to only one being. Owing to the *stuff* we are all made of, that would be an impossibility. We all share in this Liquid Love, this Divine Embrace, this energy of Oneness.

You know that Love is an exchange from heart to heart and, as Paul says, cannot be blocked or prevented. We all share; we all have access—Light Beings in Light and Light Beings incarnate. If we were to update Paul's words, the only thing necessary to add would be this: "There is nothing that can separate you from the Love of God except your choice not to believe in your own Divinity." Despite actions to the contrary, no one can separate you from Unity consciousness unless you yourself exit that portal and slide back into Separation consciousness. And even then, you are still in Union, although unaware.

The more Love is shared, the more it grows and spreads its fragrance everywhere. The more Love is shared, the more you and God become

One, and you recognize the powerful meaning invested in the words "Made in the image and likeness of God."

This is so beautifully summarized by the Indian saint Meher Baba. While on Earth, he once said, "All existence is within you. God is within you. To know God as God you must learn to love yourself as God loves you. You and God remain divided by nothing other than the veil of you yourself. I give you my blessing that you no longer subscribe to this notion of duality. When you discover you and God are One, then you discover there was never any separation to begin with."

50. Claim Your Seat as a Cosmic Creator

I have Danielle Rama Hoffman to thank for this title, as she brings in the teachings of Thoth, my precious brother in Spirit, Ancient Wisdom Keeper, and Manager of the Akashic records. Although you may realize that the gist of our efforts is a joint process of Creation, still, taking on the role of Creator yourself may be pushing the envelope. You may fear you're stepping on the toes of the "Mighty Creator, blessed is He." However, that's simply a hurdle to be overcome.

What would be different in life if you fully accepted responsibility, acknowledging that you, too, are Creator and that we're all in this together? There might be some grunts and groans, a sense of disbelief or caution, or the fear that you've extended too far beyond your comfort zone. But hopefully you'd come to appreciate your role. Perhaps you'd be less willing to blame others for a world that displeases you and more willing to help make the necessary changes. You'd be galvanized into action even before you heard the summons "All hands on deck!"

But there's also the thrill of acknowledgment—you've been working magic all along and didn't even realize it. Magic shows up in seemingly small or unrelated ways, such as how you see a sign on the road with the perfect words to fit into that new poem you've been creating or when someone calls you offering to mow your lawn after you took a bad fall or when you sense the call-waiting is exactly the call you've been waiting for.

There's no need to play small anymore; you can pride yourself on stepping into a bigger game and enjoying a delightful new process. And of course, today there's plenty of information circulating in the world, outlining the steps or keys to help you with the magic show you're creating. Consider, for a moment, how you came across that lovely new home you're in. What called you, as a physician, to suddenly turn your attention to the law? Or for that matter, what made you pick up without warning and move to a new city?

Great pivotal moments came about because you planned and dreamed and eventually lined up energetically to magnetize these new events and encounters. It's not humdrum, everyday kind of stuff; it is you exercising your role as Cosmic Creator. Once you take stock of your capabilities, you have the opportunity to position yourself more carefully and deliberately on the path to your greater purpose.

We are all in this together. (Have I said this before?) The universe keeps expanding as a result of our joint efforts. Each one born into earthly life has a task not only in evolving your own consciousness but also in adding to and up-leveling the consciousness of the planet as a whole. Did you not know your light was spreading out in all directions? We can see the twinkling light of your awakened consciousness shining like a Beacon, searching for your counterparts in Light across the Universe.

Afterword

You have heard it said. You have listened, and you have received. Join with me now in Cocreation, bringing forth a New World Order, a New Harmony, a new twist on the "Love thy Neighbor" theme.

The time is ripe for us to drop the Old Paradigm of fear, hatred, separation, and tribal consciousness. Instead, step into a new engagement, honoring the Soul's longing to live from a place of peace, generosity, kindness, courage, and palpable enduring Love. This is the Good News—the Twenty-First-Century Gospel calling for us to accept the reality that we ARE all one. Any other choice can no longer be a match for the Soul's inner longing.

This is the Evolution that you have been waiting for. Come. Take and eat in remembrance of us all; this is the Paradigm of Love. Drink the cup of the New Covenant, honoring the awakening available for everyone. Each of us is borne out of the Lineage of Love. Finally, the time has come to reclaim it. Headed in the same direction, we are bringing forth the inheritance promised to us through the ages—fully immersed, fully reciprocated, and fully saturated in the joy of Living Love. Enter the Sanctuary of your Heart and rest there awhile. Listen to the inner urge. Then with keys to your Sacred mission on Earth, go forth in peace, joy, and love to spread the Good News everywhere.

Postscript

Although Jesus gave the last word or at least the Afterword to this work, I, too, feel compelled to get a word in edgewise—or at this point, after-wise—as his scribe and editor. It is still a source of wonder and astonishment to me to have engaged in such a sacred undertaking. It arrived in bulk form and emptied itself out through my mind, my heart, my understanding, and my spirit—all of which felt as if they'd been lovingly hijacked by Jesus to be put to good use. Even though I understand that my eclectic religious and spiritual background may have influenced his choice to cocreate with me, still my mind cannot possibly wrap itself around his decision. I'm learning that some things must be left to mystery, unsolved even to this day. Yet out of millions who worship him and millions more who resonate with his teachings, how could it possibly come down to me to continue his legacy? The answer is simple. It's not. In fact, there are multiple hints throughout this transmission that I am one vehicle among many, because the work of cocreation is eternal and continually evolving and must be translated into as many backgrounds, contexts, and experiences as can accommodate this new reality—this Paradigm of Love.

Even at this juncture, it is foolish to consider the work complete. Ironically enough, once I had turned this material in to the publisher, I was awakened once again in the middle of the night with another block of thought, another round of his ideas, which made me understand how the legacy is endless and continuously self-renewing. In his prior incarnation, Jesus was iconoclastic to the extreme. He has not stopped being that way, but now he's calling us all into the *ring*, so to speak, to put paid to our old ideas and concepts. Any excuse we use as a means of remaining separate from others has expired. For if we are indeed moving into a new era in consciousness, then we are called to be in relationship in a whole new way, truly caring for and connecting with each and every Being, with no one left out. Anything less than that is antithetical to both the letter and spirit of this Paradigm of Love, and each of us is crucial to its success; in fact, you may consider this Gospel his plea that *we join together* in this bold new undertaking. You are needed to help forge new connections. You are needed to unearth creative solutions for life on the planet and to wholeheartedly bring love into the picture—everywhere.

No Gospel is perfect. But each one gives us insight into the potential for a more meaningful faith journey. What will you write? How will you serve? In what way can your gifts and talents be engaged for the benefit of humanity? Let us join with Jesus now. As he called out earlier in this Gospel, "All hands on deck."

Acknowledgments

As editor and transcriber, Jo Ann wishes to honor the following people, who directly or indirectly influenced and contributed to the emergence of this Gospel.

First to be acknowledged is **Pastor Brent Damrow** of the First Congregational Church, UCC of Stockbridge, Massachusetts, for his relentless pursuit of knowledge, his clear exegesis of Scripture, and his deep love and devotion to his congregants, which, altogether, has served as the true Template of Church. In both his tenacious pursuit of Christ's teachings and movement toward fully embodied discipleship, he has lit up not only the congregation and the town but also all of us whose hearts and minds are truly open to the kind of love and service exemplified by the Gospels.

Second to be acknowledged is **Danielle Rama Hoffman**, amazing teacher, Light worker, and channel for Thoth and the Council of Light. Through her seminal works, she has brought alive the ancient Mystery traditions and the amazing capacity we all have to connect with our Spirit Guides and Light Beings in Light. I am forever indebted to this precious sister and Devotee, who, through her unusual abilities, has channeled wisdom teachings in a penetrating and fully interactive manner and has literally helped awaken the connections within me that made this work possible.

Love and Appreciation also are extended to **Caroline Herberger, Peggy Mainor, Lena Glockner,** and **Tara Dunion** for their gracious support, cheerleading qualities, and participation in an amazing awakening process that occurred in Southern France in the fall of 2019, courtesy of Danielle's Divine Light Activation seminar.

Love and Appreciation go to **Jan Seward**, who helped assure the "birthing process" would proceed unhindered through her clairvoyant and astrological predictions and great heart of Love. The same is true for **Paula Green** and **Jim Perkins**, who were the first to read this work and then encourage me to birth and bring it forth into the world.

Love and Appreciation go out to the sweet Levitt family, especially to **Marjory and Joel**, who have loved and put up with their errant sister and her countless journeys through unorthodox and unexpected spiritual destinations. And still they invite me home for the holidays!

For extraordinary help in midwifing and producing this book, thanks are due to the amazing and creative staff of **Xlibris,** especially **Travis Black, Joy Daniels, Mark Valmoria, Sheena Genson and Jamaica Delfin**. Additional kudos to my dear friend, **Cristina Velez** for her miraculous support in translating this book from English into Spanish.

And finally, My deepest thanks and heartfelt devotion go to **Thoth, the Council of Light,** and the **Holy and Loving presence of Jesus**, who made himself known to me long ago and surprised me greatly with his love and trust in my ability to navigate this scribing process and bring forth his timely message. I am forever blessed in our Sacred Connection.

About the Editor

Jo Ann Levitt is the chief scribe and editor of these pages. She has an eclectic background in religion and spiritual practices. Brought up in the Reform Jewish tradition, she trained as a Sunday school teacher at Gratz College in Philadelphia. Later dedicating eighteen years to yoga practice and life in an ashram outside of Philadelphia, she was drawn to the austerities and emphasis on meditation and spiritual practice. She has studied Scripture from many traditions and has also had training in Peruvian shamanism as presented through Don Oscar Miro Quesada and the Heart of the Healer tradition. Forever drawn to the mystical teachings of Christ, she converted to Christianity in 2013. She also has studied and worked with Danielle Rama Hoffman and the teachings of Thoth, along with the Rose Panel Light Beings, which include Jesus; Mother Mary; Mary Magdalene; Anna, Grandmother of Jesus; Thoth; Isis; Osiris; and multiple others.

Author of *Sibling Revelry: 8 Steps to Successful Sibling Relationships* (with Marjory and Joel Levitt), published by Dell in 2001, and editor of *Pilgrim of Love: The Life and Teachings of Swami Kripalu*, published by Monkfish Book Publishers in 2004, Jo Ann continues to teach meditation and provide spiritual counseling. She holds a Master's in Education and an RN degree and is a Healing Touch practitioner and Energy worker.

Notes

The following sources can be referred to in evaluating the sages and wisdom keepers mentioned by Jesus within these pages. So as not to crowd the actual text with numbers or footnotes, the chapters with references are simply listed here in order, with keynotes and resources ascribed to the particular authors who've been quoted.

Chapter 3: What It Means to Cocreate

The term *Vasudhaiva Kutumbakam* comes from India and the yogic tradition and refers to "one world united." Found in the Maha Upanishad, the English translation is as follows:

> *This is mine, that is his, say the small minded,*
> *The wise believe that the entire world is one family.* (Maha Upanishad, 6.71–75)

Chapter 5: How Is It That We CoCreate?

The term **Sudra** (pronounced *Shudra*) once referred to the lowest class in India. The Sudra were traditionally common laborers. They could serve as slaves to higher castes, or they could take on jobs in unskilled trades. The Sudra were typically segregated from the other castes and had to use different temples and public facilities.

Chapter 8: Get a New Prescription for Your Glasses

The full quote taken from **Martin Luther King's Letter** from Birmingham Jail in 1963 is as follows: *"History will have to record that* *the greatest tragedy of this period of social transition was not the strident clamor of the bad people, but the appalling silence of the good people. Injustice anywhere is a threat to justice everywhere. We are caught in an inescapable network of mutuality, tied in a single garment of destiny. Whatever affects one directly, affects all indirectly. He who passively accepts evil is as much involved in it as he who helps to perpetrate it. He who accepts evil without protesting against it is really cooperating with it."*

Chapter 10: Compassion

Carlos Castaneda's quote is taken from **The Wheel of Time.** See also his later work **The Active Side of Infinity.**

"May I Be Happy" quote: Please see extensive notes, practices, and explanation of **Metta**, a Sanskrit word for loving-kindness. His Holiness the Dalai Lama introduced multiple phrases in prayer form to bring peace and love to the world. To learn more about the teachings of Metta, log on to the official website: https://www.dalailama.com/teachings/training-the-mind.

Chapter 12: Gathering as Disciples

St. Teresa of Avila was a sixteenth-century Carmelite nun, devotee of Christ, and prolific writer. Many of her poems and commentary are in her **Collected Works**, as well as in the **Interior Castle**. In addition, consult Mirabai Starr's translation of St. Teresa's autobiography, **Teresa of Avila: The Book of My Life.**

Antoine de Saint Exupéry (1900–1944) wrote the famous children's book **The Little Prince**, from which this quote was adapted.

Chapter 17: Prayer

Amidah contains standard Hebrew prayers and other additions according to the focus of the congregation. This prayer was offered in the

Rosh Hashanah service in September 2019 by Tikkun Olam Chavurah and Fringes, a feminist, non-Zionist organization in Philadelphia.

Chapter 20: The Nature of Sin

For Rumi's verse, see Coleman Barks's *The Essential Rumi*. He has provided a wealth of insight, careful translation, and poetic rendering of the bulk of Rumi's poetry and verse.

Chapter 27: The Lord's Prayer

Bobby McFerrin has reinterpreted many texts and poems, particularly this powerful rendition of Psalm 23, with all references to God as female. See www.bobbymcferrin.com.

Mark Miller has created a beautiful update on the Lord's Prayer, which shifts the notion of **kingdom** to that of **kin-dom**. See http://www.markamillermusic.com/.

"These boots are made for walking" is from the song of the same name by Nancy Sinatra.

Chapter 28: Swaddling Clothes

On September 8, 2019, Pastor Brent offered the sermon *Swaddled* based on Psalm 139:1–6, 13–18. This sermon was delivered at the First Congregational Church of Stockbridge, and you can listen to it online by logging on to www.stockbridgeucc.org.

Chapter 34: Sacraments

For a more detailed description of embodiment in regard to the Sacraments, see Richard Rohr's new work, *The Universal Christ*.

This Sufi Song is part of the Sikh Scripture known as **Guru Granth Sahib** and was sung as an early morning prayer by many Light Beings, including Guru Nanak, Guru Angad, Guru Amar Das, and Guru Ram Das, among others.

Chapter 36: Contemplation

Thomas Merton, famous Trappist Monk, author, and contemplative and religious thought leader, lived from 1915 until 1968. Consult *What Is Contemplation?* Also, refer to *Contemplation in a World of Action,* as well as *The Inner Experience* and *The Hidden Ground of Love.*

Chapter 39: Grace

The mention of Esther Hicks and the channeled work of Abraham can be found in books, tapes, and seminars. See www.abraham-hicks.com.

Renée Zellweger's famous line occurred toward the end of the film *Jerry Maguire*.

Chapter 42: Peace

Verses on the Faith-Mind by Seng-Ts'an, Third Chinese Patriarch, as translated by Richard B. Clarke, can be found in entirety on www.mendosa.com/way.html.

Chapter 43: On Being Present

See Eckhart Tolle's grand oeuvre *The Power of Now*. Tolle is a renowned spiritual teacher, lecturer, and author of many works, including *A New Earth: Awakening to Your Life's Purpose.*

Chapter 44: By Whose Authority?

See the compiled work *Showings* for Julian of Norwich's famous words.

Chapter 49: On Love and Holiness

"All existence is within you" quotation is taken from the work of Meher Baba (1894–1969), entitled *God Speaks.*

Chapter 50: Claim Your Seat as a Cosmic Creator

Danielle Rama Hoffman has produced three seminal works: *The Temples of Light*, *The Council of Light*, and *The Tablets of Light* (with more on the way). See her website: www.DivineTransmissions.com.

All quotes from the Gospels are taken from the New Oxford Annotated Bible, NRSV (New Revised Standard Version), 2010

CPSIA information can be obtained
at www.ICGtesting.com
Printed in the USA
LVHW031351070721
692093LV00002B/234